evolved book

about success

the most

ever known

Frame

Mr. E Dan Smith III

"ReFrame"
Authored by: Mr E. Dan Smith, III
ISBN 978-0-615-98495-7

Published by: EaseUp, Life is Heart
Boulder, CO 80302
www.lifeisheart.org

Head New Myth ReFramer: Paul Brubaker
Heart Expansion Coordinator: Heather L. Porter
Lead Instigators: Stephen Supertramp
& Reese Myra Murphy
Book Design: Mr. E. Dan Smith, III
Pre Editorial: Maribeth Flanagan
Cover Art: Dustin Brunson
Photo Credit: Minne Belger
Art Credit: Kait DeMent

Contents

Dedication

Minnie

A Foolish Note From The Author

To bring you this book, I gave God a new name, traveled through the galaxy, disappeared into the Evermore, and bent time and space to save my daughter's life.

I built a wishing fountain, constructed labyrinths, produced forgiveness music and conversed with trees.

I swam with dolphins, married myself and received darshan from Mister SPAM.

I added new words to the self-help & spiritual lexica and expect to be ridiculed. If so, then perhaps I have done my job well;)

All of this adds up to a book that I never intended to write but ended up much better than I could have planned.

This is my New Myth. These places exist, the people are real and the stories are true with a few slight embellishments.

I'd like to thank everyone who contributed to this book and my life – for I AM truly grateful for everyone with whom I have had the great fortune to meet and learn from along the way.

I don't know where the play of my life goes from here, nor do I have any advice for you. I only have questions. But through my musings, perhaps you'll allow yourself to feel something you've never felt before.

If you become offended - relax, take a deep breath and reFrame your perception of Self. It's not personal, never was and never will be.

lovE

The Fool Himself

Act I

ReFrame Zero

I AM Eternal Evermore

Ever Looked Back at Life and Seen the Perfection?

My father and I live in different mansions.

He lives in Colonial Hall.

I live in Sky Temple.

It's his first house.

    It's my most recent house.

Colonial Hall is in the Southeastern United States. She is a Queen gracing a boulevard of prominence, surrounded by magnolia, dogwood and tulip poplars and built in the late 1920's. She has perfectly manicured gardens, iconic two story columns, stucco walls, wrought iron fencing and gates. Large paintings of ancestors watch every move as visitors waltz through her large rooms. Everything has its place and an accompanying story. She is a tribute to Southern heritage.

> Sky Temple is in the Western United States. She is nouveau, perched upon a mountain overlooking a valley of lodge pole pine and a city beyond, built in the late 1990's. She has countless altars, hiking trails, a fairy circle, a wishing fountain and a labyrinth. She sits on a wild tract of land, untethered, raw and potent. She invites you to dance and move to the rhythm of all the deities present in her spaces. She is an altar to an emerging New Myth.

Colonial Hall is the kind of place where luncheons are catered, silver is polished and cars are parked for you. Things are done here the right way... most certainly.

Sky Temple is the kind of place where laughter
roars, love reigns and dreams are hatched. Things
happen in the moment and are unpredictable.

Colonial Hall is the one thing my father always
knew he wanted, even as a boy. He has never
lived anywhere else.

Sky Temple sat empty for years, and once while
visiting friends for dinner, she opened her arms
to me and I moved in.

Colonial Hall has been the home to only one family.

Sky Temple houses a community of families.

Every Sunday, my father drives from Colonial Hall to
church to worship from the same pews as his parents
and their parents. It's exactly the drive he and his
father would drive on the way to work every day of
their careers. Our family name is emblazoned on the
wall of the foyer of the large stone building. My father
is always welcome. There is a place for his hat.

As a child in the WWII-era in the South, my father
wasn't allowed to use the front stairs or be in the
downstairs living area of Colonial Hall unless he was
invited and was standing quietly in a suit. Never
imagining he had much of a choice, he went right into
his father's line of work and stayed home.

"*Life is Hard*," my father would tell me.

"*And when you truly accept that, it becomes easier.*"

I remember the day he told me he didn't enjoy his work. I was watching him get ready amongst the rack of ties, rows of dark suits and polished shoes, with all the curiosity of an eight year-old boy. I may have been one of only a few people with whom he ever shared this. It probably just slipped out.

It's not that he wasn't adept at his career, or perfectly suited. It just wasn't always his heart's choice.

My deep sense about the man is he always imagined himself in the pulpit. As he passed church on the way to work, I believe he wished to have been a Pastor.

He would have been brilliant, for at his core there is something deeply spiritual which he has learned to satisfy in nature.

It was my father who taught me about trees. He would always stop on the highway driving, in the woods hiking, in the yard working and on vacation playing to point out them out. "Wow, look at the trees," he would say. "***Would you just look at those trees***"!

My siblings and I made fun of him for that, always rolling our eyes upward and begrudgingly looking in the direction of "those trees."

Today however, when I return to his mansion, I offer him the opportunity to walk the estate grounds and share with me about all the trees in the yard. My father possesses the qualities of extraordinary vision and patience I have learned to appreciate over the years.

For example, he knows just when and where to plant which kind of trees so they are in the perfect place decades later as other trees finish their life cycle. He forms relationships with these trees, and they respond to him in kind. His relationship with the rest of the grounds of Colonial Hall is the same, with every shrub, brick, rose and flowerbed.

My father explores his heart courageously and quietly through nature, and everyone who visits his garden receives a supreme gift - finding renewal and peace. They leave inspired.

You see it is my father who manicures his gardens.

And it is I who manicures mine.

When I was born, my father and I were given a challenge. However, neither of us was told about the challenge. We had to live it out.

<u>Our challenge</u>: To learn to love the other completely despite every possible symptom of our radical differences. We could set one another free with this kind of love.

<u>My father's challenge</u>: Raise a child who would break almost every code of conduct you personally hold to be proper but who would be so charismatic that he would be impossible not to love. And when his choices strike you as most unstable, improbable, offensive and reckless, find deep trust in his life path because in the end, it is a version of your dream all along.

> <u>My challenge</u>: To emerge from tradition and cultural expectations to become an evolutionary guide of a new kind of 'church,' which reFrames most of what I was taught about religion, success, love, money, power and relationship, <u>and</u> to recognize and appreciate my family and heritage as the perfect springboard for my life's mission.

It's taken me most of my life to fully appreciate the gifts of my father: persistence, vision, wisdom, patience, trees, love of nature and gardening.

I now recognize he played his role perfectly. He did the absolute best he could, and I got exactly what I needed. He is, in fact, an extraordinary gift giver - always has been. I simply needed to become appreciative of the challenges our relationship presented to see the truth.

In this reframing of my old perception that 'we were against one another,' a universe of possibility has revealed itself.

I now see our differences as a great gift: a propelling force, rather than something to oppose.

And that, my friends, is the game we are here to play. It doesn't matter who you are, where you have come from or how colorful your past. What matters is this: are you willing to reFrame your perception of life to receive all Her gifts?

Because in all tension there is power, and within every problem, there is opportunity. Every relationship, every situation, every circumstance brings us an opportunity to reFrame difficulty, hardship and suffering. The bigger the challenge, the more extraordinary the gifts are for you – and for us all.

Are you willing to reFrame...

Judgment into Appreciation?
Depression into Self-Love?
Fear into Potential?
Anger into Power?
&
Suffering into Awakening?

Since I authored The Evolutionary Guidebook in 2009, I have been exploring new ways for humanity to set a sustainable course for the generations beyond.

I have discovered we can ALL get what we ALL want.

Yes, each of us can have everything we desire. We don't have to fight about it, nor is there a price tag. We don't have to judge or condemn anyone for it, nor do we have to hide our shame any longer. We can stop playing these "this is mine and that is yours" games. We can stop stockpiling resources and putting up walls.

Because, the last time I checked, Planet Earth has an abundance of everything already. The conditions we imagine for receiving are not real. Everything we could ever desire is now here. It is already provided for us. Our only lack is self-compassion.

And since we all have a human heart, self-compassion is simply a matter of personal perception. It is self-love that allows us to receive the gifts of the Father – we just have to reFrame in order to see things in this light.

Rather than remaining in resistance to this truth, we can take the energy of opposition and use it to open the heart to begin *reFraming* our perception. It all begins and ends, with the heart.

ReFraming

The Process of Shifting Perspective to Receive the Gifts of Life <u>Without</u> Condition.

Converting Resistance into Compassion.

Manifesting by Way of Subtraction.

ReFraming allows us to quickly become the change we have been seeking. We can see how everything and everyone has been perfectly placed here and now, and how everything we need is already present.

Suddenly, success isn't something to obtain, nor is it something to manifest. Success becomes very simple.

Success is Compassion.

A compassionate person no longer tries to gain anything. A compassionate person seeks to release any illusion of separation, condition and scarcity, in order to receive exactly what is in alignment with their highest good. They continually explore the question: *How Can I Serve?*

ReFraming lifts a veil to reveal how we each affect the entire matrix of human consciousness with our compassionate perspective, much like waves moving through the ocean to impact distant shores.

We suddenly see the vitality and importance of every human being, which sends powerful waves of love into the sea of humanity, causing an expansion of wakefulness in all people.

This new awareness comes with a new inspired sense of responsibility. We are naturally inspired to consciously reFrame with others to amplify compassion for a sustainable, peaceful and abundant existence for all.

This is our gift.

It is our time.

We can literally love the old paradigms into new opportunities for humanity. We don't have to oppose anyone or anything any longer.

We can move from separation and division into cooperation, connection and collaboration – simply by loving people and situations as they are, without any need to actively change them using traditional modalities.

We can move from revolution to simply... evolution.

It all begins and ends with our heart.

So, let's journey into this book together and *reFrame*. It is safe, my friends. Come out and play.

All is Provided for Now

<u>Note</u>: At each chapter end, there are four frames.

You'll need to turn the book counter-clockwise to read the frames, starting at bottom left.

Imagine you are opening to a new perspective as you explore the questions with willingness and curiosity.

Take your time.

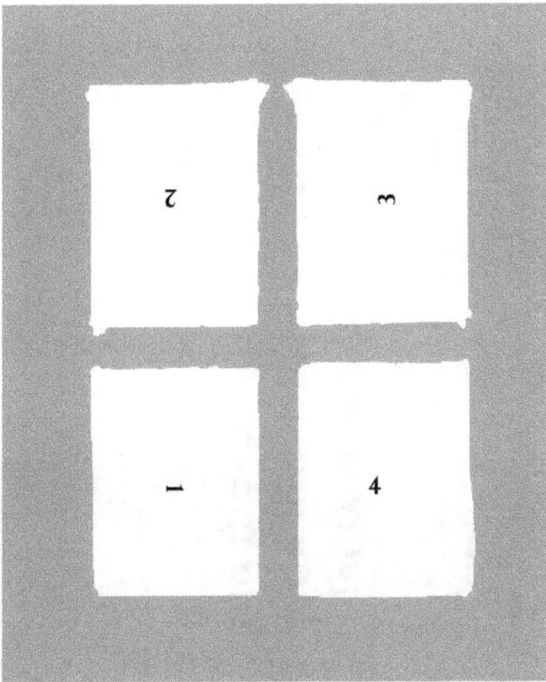

Can we shift our reality when we love what is?

As we shift, won't others shift along with us?

Life doesn't have to be hard, does it?

Life is Heart.

ReFrame One

Mister SPAM Man

Ever Had A Simple Trip Turn Into An Epic Journey?

I have just stepped onto a plane for the six-hour flight from Los Angeles to Kona, Hawaii.

In what seems like an eternity after only 30 minutes, I am uncomfortably realizing I slept too much last night and have nothing to entertain myself. I'm not a drinker and the couple next to me is asleep.

The only light in the cabin comes from flickering screens and the edges of drawn shades against the rising sun. My body is fidgety and tense, reflecting a sense of uneasiness I have yet to reconcile. Wanting to relax into the flight and let everything go, I take a deep breath into my heart to open to the coming adventure.

I am traveling from Colorado to the Big Island of Hawaii for the wedding of my dear friends and community housemates, Soma and Q.

But this trip is not what is pecking at my awareness in the cramped space 44,400 feet above the Pacific Ocean. What won't leave me alone right now is the question surfacing in these moments of forced contemplation:

> *How do I utilize my gifts to model a new*
> *pathway of success for humanity to travel?*

A version of this question has been plaguing me for the last decade or more. It seems like the more I recognize my gifts, the more unclear the answer.

These aren't traditional gifts; they are a bit out of the range of 'normal.' Even my mother knew she hadn't understood my motives just before she died of cancer at age 43. Near the end, she confided in her friend, "*I wish I hadn't tried to fit that boy into a square hole.*"

Yes, my life has been nothing short of an ongoing exploration of foolishness and inner desire, binding me between a new world of success and the global version of community my heart keeps telling me is possible.

It's been a journey beyond societal norms, pressing against any and all outer boundaries into empty space. I have felt pigeonholed while answering the call to explore; my emerging wings fluttering awkwardly somewhere between safety and peril.

And, here it is again… angst; churning and arising within me in seat 4D.

It is the inner knowing I must move 'all-in' to live completely in accordance with who I am authentically - a pioneer of sorts in a human evolutionary movement already underway.

There is no doubt this is my soul's calling, but the route is elusive, mysterious and terrifying. Surely the most enlightening path would be to live my life and just let everyone and everything be as is. However, my soul keeps calling. And the voice is getting louder.

Little do I know how the first few hours in Hawaii will reFrame my entire life and inspire me into a newly evolved collaborative space of empowerment for myself, and perhaps for others.

I sigh, close my eyes and find restless sleep.

Walking through the Kona airport, it is with both a sense of relief and celebration as I embrace the soon-to-be-married couple.

We are here to participate in a Sacred Union marriage of higher consciousness. Others are on the way too. It isn't just my housemates getting married. We are all marrying ourselves; by bringing together the divine masculine and feminine aspects of ourselves.

This union of recalling forgotten aspects of our true selves helps us embody a higher spiritual frequency as we step more fully into personal empowerment and humanitarian service. These are my people. I can be fully me. My heart expands with this awareness.

Over lunch, Q explains the best way to acclimate into Hawaii is simply to jump right into the ocean and go snorkeling.

"No better time than now," I say.

We walk to the car.

The drive to the beach is surreal.

It's a road I have been down before.

Once. Maybe.

I'm not sure.

Pulling into the parking lot, I am enveloped in a suspended state of curiosity. "Is this the exact same spot I nearly died in heavy surf eleven years ago?" I ask myself.

"It couldn't possibly be... could it?" I answer.

Seeing the tiny beachside church confirms my hunch.

"Oh wow, it is!"

The ocean scene today is vastly different from the day I nearly died. The water is calm and clear. There are people quietly getting in and out with snorkeling gear. This in stark contrast to the last time I was here, when chaos reigned supreme.

Saying nothing about the past and opening to the curiosity inside, I fumble with the mask and fins and awkwardly wade into the bay with my snorkeling gear. The feeling of my body slipping into the water and the excitement of a new adventure shifts me into an entirely different awareness.

The expansive life of color and peacefulness astounds me. I am immersed in the underwater life, following a sea turtle amongst the coral and fishes and deeply feeling the connection of the entire ecosystem. I am humbled by the perfection of everything coexisting peacefully. Here, I drop even more fully into my heart.

I feel different when I emerge from the water. More empowered, free.

Drying off, I mention to Q how the ocean nearly took my life eleven years ago.

He immediately suggests, "Walk down the beach and conduct a *soul retrieval*, just in case you left a part of yourself on the beach."

Q is a man of potent wording and exact timing. He is gifted with a propensity for inquiring with the right question at the precise moment a new direction is calling your soul. He couldn't just live with anyone. One has to be able to take his medicine.

Now on any other day and at any other place, I might be more inquisitive about how to actually conduct soul retrieval. This is a new venture for me.

But today... well, today is different. Come on now. If Neale Donald Walsh can suddenly have "Conversations with God," I can certainly guide myself through an impromptu soul retrieval.

I immediately turn and walk intentionally toward the tiny church. Everything seems to be happening more slowly. The colors are louder, sounds clearer and the sun brighter as I imagine the potential of reclaiming a lost part of myself.

Arriving at a spot that feels appropriate for ceremony, I plant my feet into the sand, take some deep breaths into my belly and extend my arms outward into a cross formation. Lifting my chin, I lean back to stretch my chest and open my heart.

From this posture, I hold the intent of inviting all empowering aspects of myself to return.

Moments later, I feel an expansion within my heart. A golden rod of light opens in the Heavens and runs into the crown of my head, while the exact same thing happens from the Earth below the sand into my feet and legs. My heart is the nexus point of these twin energies. An expanded column of energy, light and love envelops me.

My feet are still planted in the sand. I am still here on the beach, and yet my awareness is transported back to this very spot eleven years earlier, apparently to witness my near-death experience in a new way.

That occurrence was in 2002.

I was called to be with my guru for a ten-day trip of volunteer work and spiritual practice at his yoga and meditation retreat center. The retreat center is located in the hills above the bay. I spent my days deeply immersed in the community and toiling in the sun above the shoreline.

25

As Sunday approached - the only day I had free - there was a growing desire in me to surf. As fate would have it on this particular Sunday, the waves were eight to fifteen feet high.

What a curious experience to witness one's self.

I am here on the beach now, and simultaneously with my younger self here, and then.

I observe my younger self nearby surveying the ocean. I see how his determination to surf is coloring his awareness to overlook every external and internal reason to stay out of the water. I feel the strength of his will.

He is a **f**ool.

Peering through the lens of his foolish perspective, the waves still look surfable. From my vantage point now, they clearly do not.

I watch the fool walk to the beachside surf shop and stretch the truth about his surfing expertise to convince the owner to rent him a board. As the likelihood of certain death is explained to him, I hear him say smugly, "I'm a professional. I have surfed waves like this before."

Recognizing rationale as fruitless, the surf shop operator walks the younger man outside and points towards the bay.

"The rip current is strong with these giant waves, strong enough to take you to Japan or kill you. Make sure to stay on the bay side of the little church. Otherwise you'll be taken on a ride and smashed between the waves and the rocks."

The fool eagerly places the surfboard under his arm and walks to the same spot in which now I stand, and pauses as if to survey the ocean.

In the pause, I join him.

We paddle into the surf as one. It's exactly as I remember. He is strong and moves through the broken waves with ease. Then turning to face the shore, he catches the first breaking wave all the way to the beach. I can feel the triumph in him. He is smiling and now feels more confidence than fear.

Little does he know, a set of much larger waves are headed for the bay.

My heart reaches out to hold us both.

The fool paddles back out toward the breaking waves. I help him as much as I can. As I open to the innocence of being nearly drowned once again, I am present to his innocence of the approaching Z-Energy.

Z-Energy

An Unseen 'Wave' Dramatically Altering Life.
A Blessing in Disguise

I Never Saw It Coming... *Is Usually Said*
as the Reality of the Diagnosis, Accident,
Disaster, Affair or Situation Becomes Real.

He certainly doesn't see the giant wall of whitewater coming until it is too late. Suddenly he is grasping for anything that feels like air, tumbling under the water as though he is in a washing machine. There is no up or down. I feel his lungs burning, mind racing and heart pounding.

Every time he surfaces, he is instantly plowed under by another wave and then another and then another, barely keeping enough air in his lungs.

I am calmly experiencing this again for his first time. He is fighting for our life, but I know "we" survive.

Finally surfacing after the set of waves has passed, he pulls at the surfboard still tethered to his ankle. Emerging from battle, the fool slumps his torso safely over the board, with one eye surveying the scene.

Catching the tiny church on the beach whizzing past and seeing the waves crashing on the rocks coming quickly closer, I feel his surrender. He isn't giving up, however. He is giving over his desire to survive to God.

His desire is strong.

I feel pulsing energy flowing, and watch him shift quickly to paddle position and begin chanting the sacred prayers of the spiritual retreat center. I feel his heart focus on the intent of returning home.

From my expanded perspective, I notice while he is lying on the board chanting the sacred mantra, his spiritual energy expands vertically like mine on the beach. He is supported by Heaven & Earth.

An energy field blossoms from within the center of his chest expanding outward. I feel both of us in this vertical column of energy. The space around us is immediately affected and everything begins organizing itself around our shared intent to survive.

At this moment, I am as much of the <u>Fool</u> as I have ever been.

Suddenly, I notice everything slows down and we are at peace in the chaos, riding the board in the rip current with neither fear nor panic. The rocks, which moments ago looked menacing, summon us. The once monstrous waves are playful and light.

I remember however, what is was like back then. Everything was happening in a blur. It was pure chaos. Twice I had looked into the eyes of mortality.

Sensing the exact right moment, he paddles us towards the rocks with every ounce of willpower he can muster. We land with the energy of a wave, which sets the fool down gently enough on the large rocks for him to survive with only minor cuts.

He scrambles out of the reaches of the next wave to collect himself. Dazed and slightly cut, but mostly okay, he shuffles a few hundred yards back to the surf shop. The board is fine.

Only 20 minutes has passed between renting and returning the board, but an eternity has passed between us. Drenched in seawater and licking his wounds, my younger self is not victorious. Dripping in blood, he sheepishly returns the surfboard and is in deep judgment of himself for almost dying. He feels terribly irresponsible.

The column of energy is gone from him, yet it remains in me. He averts his eyes from the Man who rented him the board. He is ashamed.

I see anger, confusion and self-hatred swell in his abdomen in the form of a pulsing maroon flame. Not knowing what to do, he walks outside to the beach. His emotions get the best of him and he makes a vow to never let ego be in charge again.

A bright light leaves him and disappears into the ocean. I can see he just threw away more than ego. He tossed his confidence too. The maroon flame retracts into his abdomen, flickering just below the surface of his awareness – and yet shining brightly all the same. He is in shock.

As I lovingly observe this wounded aspect of myself through him, my soul retrieval begins in earnest. I feel the egocentric part of myself he just dismissed begin to make its way back into me. I send love to my younger self, struggling with his actions.

For the first time I lovingly look upon his youthful ego and recognize that this experience startled him into new appreciation of life and family. I see it as a necessary part of his journey. I forgive him for his wayward actions for the first time.

As I observe him with new eyes, I notice a brilliant star emerge from the ocean and arc above the waves.

As it begins to stream toward me, I open my heart to receive. The light penetrates my chest, and I feel a great expansion of love.

I welcome back my mojo, my moxie.

The missing part of my soul has been retrieved.

I walk slowly, almost floating, back to Q and Soma. I am feeling everything, but saying nothing as we load up our gear and drive to a large drug store up the street for some fresh water.

Entering the store, Q asks a woman to show us to the bottled water. As she guides us to the proper aisle, I stop to observe a man taking cans of SPAM out of a grocery cart to stack them on a large display which must be at least 7 feet wide and 7 feet tall.

He is beaming and sporting an impeccable blue uniform, starched shirt, a bow tie, flawless hair and an extraordinary smile.

There are thousands of cans of SPAM stacked at the end of the shopping aisle in the form of a great medieval castle. With great curiosity I watch this man place more and more cans of SPAM on the nearly completed display. I can feel his dedication.

He is surrendered to his craft, and treats this towering display of SPAM as a magnificent work of art. He is ecstatic and knows I am watching him.

Observing him play with SPAM, I reflect upon the day. I just arrived in Hawaii for lunch, snorkeled with a giant sea turtle, and reclaimed my mojo in an impromptu soul retrieval at the scene of a near-death experience I had 11 years ago – all by 4:00 PM.

And now, I am apparently participating in some sort of Sacred SPAM Ceremony.

The entire day seems to be oddly and magically self-organized without any effort on my part.

Then, in complete synchronicity with my thoughts, Mister SPAM pauses with his chest expanded and arms spread outward holding two cans of SPAM. Holding this posture powerfully, he turns his head slowly toward me and flashes a gleaming smile of perfect white teeth.

With the timing and delivery of a great comedian, he enthusiastically says; **"You Gotta Get Your SPAM Up!"** and quietly goes back to his artistry.

I stagger backwards a bit, onto my heels.

His posture and words have come together in a way that has stunned me. I feel changed all over, again.

Somehow I know every question I have ever asked has just been answered in a language I don't quite understand. Its arrival is much like a great wave of Z-energy, plowing into me and leaving me in a suspended state of shock and gasping for solid ground.

When Q returns moments later with the water, I follow him back to the car, laughing. Everything has become curiously funny.

EVERYTHING.

As we pull out of the parking lot, Q and Soma begin laughing too, even though I cannot get the words out about Mister SPAM. I keep trying to speak, but the laughter won't let me explain. It's infectious. We lose control and Soma is almost unable to drive the car. It feels as though we are in an open portal of magic, which keeps expanding wider and wider for us all.

The three of us came to be housemates nearly a year before. The spiritual mystery of life is our collective interest, and in this moment our mutual intent has brought us to joy - pure and absolute joy.

As the week progresses, *"You Gotta Get Your SPAM Up!"* becomes the daily rallying cry as we recognize the playful metaphor for raising our spiritual energy to experience joy and magical times.

SPAM

Human Energy. One's Spiritual Vibration. The Measure of the Heart's Openness.

SPAM is up…

When Everything Becomes Magical and Works Out Better Than Anyone Could Have Planned.

The Experience of Life Flowing Perfectly.

Within a few days, the rest of the wedding party arrives and we notice how our elevated SPAM is transferable and everyone is impacted. As the week progresses, there is an explosion of serendipity as our group energy becomes a dynamic force of creation.

The island keeps opening up all kinds of doors for new adventures... and nearly all are unplanned. We visit amazing places and meet extraordinary people who share their hearts and abundance with us.

It is an astonishing time together on every level.

End Act I

What if the point
of life was simply
to be in Joy?

What if getting
SPAM up was
your only plan?

What if all you had to do was open your Heart?

Would your life become an amazing journey?

Sacred Union Ceremony Site

Fool's Gold

The **Fool** (capital F) represents the viewpoint of the main character when he enjoys self-compassion, and an enlightened perspective. He is *re-Framed*.

The **fool** (lower f) represents an adopted viewpoint of suffering, shame and guilt, clouding innocence.

ReFraming is simple. Each chapter has you explore two or more stories from multiple perspectives. Utilize the f/Fool's Journey to open to a larger perspective by finding compassion for him, and therefore yourself.

The key to the reFrame experience is *to feel* things you've not allowed yourself to feel before.

The moment you feel anything, use the SPAM Stance to expand percolating emotions into a current of love. This raises SPAM, and allows the reFrame to appear.

At the end of each chapter use the reFrame questions to explore new perspectives for you and humanity. Be curious. Be inquisitive. Be courageous. And listen from your heart, deeply.

Take your time. Only a fool would hurry.

The **Maroon Flame** represents unresolved human emotion stored in the navel area, namely shame and fear. It exists in everyone and represents a hidden gate to a passage of freedom through the heart.

Act II

ReFrame Two

Your Evolutionary Guide

Haven't Guides Always Been With You In Life?

The fool is 5 years old.

He is at his family's home on a gorgeous late spring afternoon in Nashville, Tennessee.

The fool has retreated indoors after many hours playing in the sandbox.

He sits on his knees near the top of the grand spiral staircase. His arms are tucked inward, elbows down with his small hands holding tightly onto the rails of the ornate banister. His face is pressed into the space between his knuckles.

From here, he is almost removed from the large foyer but can safely observe everything happening below. He can sense an unsettled feeling of change lurking about the house. He is strategically ready for the big event. Today is the day when a new "someone" will arrive.

Fortunately he knows that his escape route is behind him and up the stairs.

His mother and father are brilliant people, graduating at the top of both their collegiate and graduate studies. They have chosen to embrace familial responsibility by raising their children in the traditional home located on a prominent street in a prestigious neighborhood.

His mother has just been called into civic duty. His parents want assistance with cleaning a large home and caring for the children while she volunteers to make their hometown a better place.

I know the fool's parents need far more than they imagine now. Their son came to earth with a specific soul blueprint that requires a lot of resources.

He has come here to reFrame the conventional wisdom held in their family, in their community and beyond. He chose his parents and they chose him. It is a shared mission of the heart but won't be an easy road. A lot of tension exists between his actions and their expectations.

From the omnipotent perch of the Fool, I observe the pieces falling together perfectly and I can see that everything the boy and his parents need is being provided for now.

There has just been a series of knocks on the front door. At first, it was just a light tapping that only the young fool could hear. This alerted him to scamper to his perch and wait.

The tapping has now become a light knocking. He hears Mommy's steps coming down the long hallway from the kitchen, pausing to let the pattering of little feet catch up.

The rapping is louder now, as the person at the door has become courageous enough to use the large brass knocker.

The young boy's grip on the banister rails becomes more intense as his mother emerges from the swinging door into the foyer and walks over the oriental rugs to open the large front door. She is holding his baby brother on her right hip, and the hand of his younger sister is wrapped around her left middle finger.

He watches his Mommy pry her hand loose to open the door and allow his sister to grip her leg instead, using the apron as a shield.

On the other side of the door, I observe a young woman trying to calm her shaking hands and nerves. She is holding the classified section of a newspaper under her arm while clutching her purse and reaching out for the knocker again with her free hand.

It took every ounce of her courage to leave the factory before the shift ended and to cross the railroad tracks into unfamiliar lands. She has prayed long and hard about this moment late into the night.

But now, standing on the large stone porch of a house bigger than the apartment project in which she lives, she can barely knock - imagining the worst of who and what might be on the other side.

From the fool's lookout, he is also wondering about who is on the other side. His feet flicker as if ready scurry to his room at any moment.

As the door opens slowly, his view is obscured by the expanding silhouette of his mother and siblings created by the bright afternoon light suddenly shining into the cavernous house.

Light is bouncing off the polished woods floors and reflecting through the crystal chandelier in prisms, giving the antebellum home a strange cathedral-esque feel.

The little boy then watches the silhouette swing to the right like a gate granting passage to a visiting dignitary. A figure slowly emerges.

She remains cloaked in light. But he sees her dark face, and hears her voice as introductions and conversation are made. There is a growing sense of relief as he feels his mother relax.

Pressing his face forward into the banister rails and squinting his eyes, the fool is full of curiosity. He strains to get a glimpse of the visitor through the veil of sunlight.

I have already seen what the boy wants to see. She is humble and strong in her faith.

She is perfect.

I know what no one else knows; this boy will need two mommas for what lies ahead, and both women will need one another in ways they cannot imagine now.

Suddenly everyone turns and all eyes land on him as the new voice asks, *"Who dat up on dem stairs?"* The light is now shining on the fool.

"This is Minnie," says his mother. "She has come to be with our family."

His cover blown, the fool tries to escape. But he cannot pry himself loose from the banister. He has lodged his head between the rails.

He is foolish indeed.

I took to Minnie well.

She encouraged me to play and be in my heart. We laughed a lot. She was the greatest gift I ever received.

Minnie was there to greet us after school and during the holidays. She would always find enough four-leaf clovers in our back yard for everyone, since no one else could seem to find any.

She taught us about the living God. She told us stories of how the Holy Spirit would move through her church pews and inspire the people to shout and dance.

Her people had fun while they praised Jesus. Her life was filled with the Spirit. She taught us about love, compassion and regular folk. Through her stories, we learned about a whole 'nother world.

Whenever we needed her, she was there.

About this time in my life, I would lay in my bed at night and travel through the galaxy. I don't ever remember not being able to do it, and yet the memory of it returned to me much later in life.

This inner exploration of space more or less happened to me, rather than being a product of my will. It wasn't a rare experience but it didn't happen all that often.

A feeling would come over my body while I was falling asleep. It would just barely keep me awake. I would turn on my back and lay with my arms and legs spread out like I was sunning myself in the sand at the beach.

Suddenly a passage would open in my chest, and I would begin flying *eternally* into outer space amongst the stars and planets.

I was everywhere and nowhere at the same time.

As I was flying through my heart into the emptiness of space, I would hear a soothing voice assuring me everything was happening perfectly, and I was safe.

I AM **Sarza**.

I AM the Earth and I AM the Evermore.

I AM the Great Mother, and I AM Nature.

I AM Provider of All, and I AM always with you.

Play and be free in your heart.

47

Over time I learned how to let go more and more and trust what was happening. I would always fall asleep after flying and the memory of it would be gone when I awoke the next morning.

Weeks or months later, I would be lying in my bed and the feeling would return, triggering my memory of Sarza, and I would go flying into the galaxy all over again.

I AM **Sarza**.

I AM available to you at all times through your heart by listening.

You will remember and guide others to listen.

Until then, know this:

All Is Provided For Now.

And then I fell asleep.

Would your life
shift to reflect
this truth?

What if you knew
life always works
out perfectly?

Would it
become easier
to reFrame?

Then would you
always have what
you needed?

ReFrame Three

The Power Paradox

How Do The Most Memorable Moments Arrive?

It's a warm and sunny winter day. The fool has just arrived home after school.

The family's plan is to leave the next day for a spring break ski trip to Aspen, CO.

Minnie is home.

His Mother is not. His Father is at work.

It is the day before the fool's twelfth birthday. He stands in the breezeway connecting the house to the garage.

In the three-car structure, his father's handmade sailboat hangs from the rafters. At least a dozen bales of hay are innocently stacked underneath.

Lawnmowers, ladders and bicycles fill the space. It's a storehouse for the family's busy life.

The fool is wearing a ski jacket for the first time in his life on a warm late winter day. He feels cool. The jacket is borrowed for the trip. Spring Break has arrived. He is happy. Adventure is in the air.

Looking toward the back yard, he places his hands into the new jacket's pockets to survey the scene. His left hand discovers a book of firecrackers.

His right finds a box of matches.

He can hardly believe his great fortune. Forbidden instruments of fun are suddenly available to him, like magic. He didn't even have to look for them.

Smiling, he walks past the garage, making a beeline for the army men and tanks in his sandbox.

The Fool knows what the fool doesn't know yet. There are more matches in his pockets than firecrackers.

A great desert battle ensues. And when the ammunition has run out, the fool walks innocently toward the garage fingering the remaining three matches. In his path at eye level, a long piece of straw beckons.

He lights the end, and immediately goes to blow it out.

But, the straw is hollow, and the force of his breath is an accelerant – blowing the flame through the tube and into the space between the bales.

In an instant the flames are over his head and rising toward the hull of the sailboat. The boy turns to grab the hose that is always hooked to the spigot at the entrance to the garage behind him.

Instead, an empty pail rests underneath.

There is nothing a Fool can do but love the fool.

He turns on the water and watches the bucket fill at a snail's pace. He can hear the crackling of the flames behind him. He urges the water to come out faster. The pail is filling slower than the flames are growing. The fool is calculating when to throw the water.

He feels the heat of the flames through the ski jacket, causing him to turn his head. He is shocked at the size of the fire.

He grabs the half-full bucket and throws the water into the center of the blaze.

The flames hiss at his foolery, and seemingly mock him by growing even more in stature. The boy backs up and sees glass breaking and falling from the open garage door. The fire is loud. The sound of chaos alerts him the situation is out of control.

The child runs inside.

"Minnie!

The garage is on fire!

The garage is on fire!

In a flash, Minnie has looked into the garage and runs back into the room. "I call 'da firemens.

You call yo Daddy!"

A few minutes later, the boy calls his father as the sound of sirens becomes audible in the background. Moments later, he is running to meet the arriving fire trucks.

People are pulling off the road on the way home from work to watch the commotion.

The young boy helps the firemen carry the large hoses through the expansive front yard.

The fire burns hot. The yard is filled with smoke. The flames are licking the side of the 4th generation home greedily.

I observe his parents arrive separately. They are concerned for their son and home, but also aware of the attention the fire is receiving from the neighbors. In their torsos, I see maroon flames expand as the chaos triggers deep and ancient emotion.

As the entire neighborhood watches, the home is spared. The handmade sailboat is gone with the wind, but the lingering smell of shame and smoke remains. It sticks to everything.

The fool runs up the street and into the forest to escape. He has been in trouble before and awaits his fate amongst the trees. I notice how his head hangs low in the fading afternoon light.

The premeditation his parents imagine does not exist in him. Colder air sweeps into the woods. His borrowed jacket keeps him warm, but he no longer feels cool.

It's the last time he will be allowed to leave the yard for six weeks, but that's not what hurts the most.

What hurts the most is fulfilling the requirement set by his father; writing a five-page paper on arson to explain why he purposefully set the garage on fire.

What the fool doesn't know is that this is a necessary exercise to help him develop strength for bigger challenges down the road.

Yes, I was that child.

I loved playing with matches, peeing outside, cutting up in the classroom, rifling through the neighbors' garages at night and exploring the woods near home.

Sitting still in school was a great challenge. I was well known for my under-achievement with the teachers and my precociousness with the administration.

Barely moving on from one grade to the next, I garnered a standing ovation at my high school graduation for acing three exams during the last week of school to earn the lowest possible passing grades.

Bless my parents. I was a tough child to supervise - a handful as they say. Had I been born a generation or two before, I may have worn the dunce cap in the corner of the classroom. Had I been born a generation or two later, I likely would have been medicated for numerous 'ailments.'

Despite the best intentions of everyone trying to help me, I was getting a message early in life... *something is wrong with you... let's fix it. You need to act a certain way.*

I believed these people, and I learned to keep my truth inside as a way to stay out of trouble. I became ashamed of myself. I found myself alternating between cultural expectations, and the natural desires of my heart. I was a fool, but couldn't appreciate my foolishness yet.

I was being pulled in two directions. I vacillated between the polarities of conformity and authenticity, adopting society's myth of one being right and the other wrong. There was tremendous inner conflict, which I learned to hide.

I got older, graduated from college somehow, moved out West and started a family. The tension only mounted with mortgages and career. I kept building upon a false pretense of myself, pressing away any and all contrary feelings beyond my awareness.

Then at age 42, a passage opened inside of my heart and I went through. Suddenly everything was different.

The journey into the heart has been nothing short of upsetting, treacherous, harrowing, unstable, erratic, wild, gut-wrenching, and extraordinarily beautiful beyond any imagining I could have ever had.

During this time I have been…

> homeless,
>
> heartbroken,
>
> bankrupt,
>
> penniless,
>
> divorced,
>
> shunned,
>
> pitied,
>
> judged,
>
> misdiagnosed with mental illness,

and been the happiest in my life.

I have been robbed in a foreign country of my wallet and passport and discovered the extraordinary truth about the consciousness of abundance, which exists just beyond our limited ideas of conditional economics.

I have inadvertently pissed people off and said goodbye to many friends, lost contact with close family and become impervious to the opinions of others.

I have been challenged at every turn and on every level about the beliefs and limitations I held as truths, only to discover a much broader matrix of consciousness supporting all of life.

I have toured the United States coast-to-coast, hitchhiked in Mexico, swam with dolphins in Hawaii, surfed in Costa Rica, journeyed deep into the Sierra and Rocky Mountains, and secretly slept in people's garages when I had nowhere else to go.

I have fallen deeply in love and been devastated when the relationships ended; each time learning something incredible that was essential to my life path.

I have left my family and yet continued to father my three extraordinary children with love and presence. I have continued to co-parent with their mother while coming to appreciate my own parents more than ever.

I have worked spiritually with hundreds of people for whatever they could afford to pay me, and seen many of them discover things that brought both them and me, great joy.

I have built a labyrinth for a mental health center so people could discover more about themselves by stepping beyond the linear framework of their conditioning.

I have initiated an evolved 'church', written two books and moved into in a fabulous community home called the Sky Temple.

I have worked with musicians to create forgiveness music and have watched people be transformed to the core of their being… including myself.

I have come to know that humanity is rising to its challenges and a new earth is being born at this very moment. And I've come to realize the most important thing any person can do is to get their SPAM Up!

My entire methodology can be summed up in the following statement:

"I have said yes to everything my heart desired and tasted the fruit of my shame to find only love."

Furthermore, I wouldn't trade a moment of my experience for anything in the world, for I have learned to get my SPAM up and reconnect to Sarza.

Sarza

The Divine Self-Organizing Field Shaping Reality Around the Quality of Your Intention.

The Giver of All.

Pure Nature.

Joy.

I have learned when SPAM is up, everything falls into natural order because Sarza only knows Divine perfection.

I believe each one of us knows Sarza already. She is both the flood and the resurrection after the flood. Sarza causes people in disasters from different backgrounds to share resources without need for compensation. She alerts the animal kingdom before the tsunami to seek higher ground.

Sarza allows everything to be created out of the empty space of nothingness. She brings sustenance to your intent, reality to your dreams, and partners for your growth.

She is the death of winter, the rebirth of spring, the hot sun of summer and the harvest in the fall. Sarza is pure perfection. She is the ever-present Divine intelligence in action, responding to recognition, intent, trust and gratitude.

She provides extraordinary gifts disguised as challenges designed to open human hearts.

She asks us to live within the following ***Power Paradox***… Be 100% responsible for everything in your life, and yet give up all control.

She is the Divine Feminine.

What if they were
told to just follow
their hearts?

What if we
never made
children wrong?

Would they find
their way into
inspiration?

Wouldn't they
grow up and
change the world?

ReFrame Four

Alter Your Awareness

At What Point Does Truth Actually Set You Free?

Riding in the covered back of a small pickup truck, the fool is now 13 years old.

A trusted chaperone is driving him back from a camping trip.

The passenger seat is empty.

It's a five-hour drive back home in the cramped space filled with boxes and suitcases. He sits facing away from the cab, staring out the side window. He is sore from sitting in the metal truck bed and unable to extend his body into a seated position.

His energy is flat and defeated. He is confused. His abdomen pulses with the maroon flame.

While stopped for gas, the sliding glass window opens from inside the front of the truck. A shadowy unshaven face appears. The fool's energy retracts, and he refuses to acknowledge the questions or even the Shadow at all.

His mind is consumed and his feelings raw. He is unsure of exactly what has transpired, but he knows one thing: it will never happen again.

As unpleasant as it seems to him now, he knows what he has to do. He is using the time alone on the road to find the right words to tell his mother what has happened.

Hours later, nearing his house, the fool has found enough courage to tell her. I observe his energy field. It has strengthened, elongated and become white.

Ready for the challenge, he presses his face against the side window of the truck bed as they approach home. In anticipation of getting out of the truck and running inside to find her, he moves toward the rear gate.

As they pull into the driveway, he sees his mother waiting in front of the rebuilt garage holding an ornately wrapped gift.

A feeling of dread overtakes him.

The Shadow parks directly in front of his mother.

As the boy watches helplessly from the pickup truck bed he cannot open himself, the Shadow emerges from the driver's seat to accept the gift of thanks. He unwraps it. It's a hot-air popcorn popper.

Mother and the Shadow are laughing. She seems elated to have been without the fool, and grateful to the Shadow.

I wish I could tell him it's not personal.

A woman with breast cancer needs time and space for nurturing.

Especially since both mommas developed breast cancer this past year. Yes, Minnie has cancer too.

By the time the Shadow lets him out of the back of the truck, the boy's resolve to reveal what happened is gone. He has seen the joy in his mother's eyes. He imagines the pain and suffering his truth might cause her.

His energy field shrinks, and I watch him push the experience away into his abdomen. The maroon flame brightens within.

He gives his mother a quick hello and disappears into the backyard to try and be a kid.

She would never know.

Two months later, the fool is sent back to Christian Summer Camp.

The Shadow is there, lurking.

Sixteen years into a marriage with three children, a career and living in my dream home, my *shame basket* can no longer contain the secret.

Life has become an up and down ride. I enjoy periods of success and happiness, but then fall back into an inner struggle.

Shame Basket

A Collection of Hidden Desires and Emotions Awaiting Appreciation and Forgiveness.

Secrets Keeping Humanity from Their Compassionate Truth, and in Dramatic Conflict.

The Barrier of Receiving Abundance.

Recently, I had committed to a daily meditation practice as an antidote and taken a spiritual teacher. Most days, sitting on that cushion at my altar, I found myself reaching deep down into the desire of my heart, asking to be free of suffering.

Like any spiritual practice, it brought my awareness to some areas of my life needing attention. I had really been struggling in my career and I wanted to know the reason. I went to see a healer of sorts. She encouraged me to begin telling the truth.

"The truth?" I said. "What do you mean?"

"Whatever truth that hasn't been told," she replied.

I knew in that moment that I had to tell her what I was unable to tell my mother.

In my youth, I attended a Christian Sports Camp.

There were lots and lots of rules at this camp. The camp was owned by a towering figure, like a skyscraper: a clean-cut white man who was unabashedly 'right wing.'

A specimen of health, athleticism and immense presence, The Man openly condemned gay people, black people, poor people and most of all lazy people. Basically, all people who didn't fit his mold of righteous.

The Man had a Deputy.

He had grey skin. He was unkempt, slightly overweight and had scraggly sideburns. His posture was slouched. He was loud and wore a whistle around his neck. He was like a Shadow of The Man.

The Man made the rules of the game.

The Shadow dealt the cards.

There was more to this camp. As long as you played by the rules, you could enjoy incredible freedoms.

We had the run of hundreds of acres containing lakes, forests, a river, fields and every human-made instrument of fun you could imagine: gymnasiums, slides, rides, games, competitions, zip-lines and shooting sports.

It was a paradise and attracted kids from all over the United States and Mexico. Many came back year after year. You either fell right in line, or became a scapegoat. There was no middle ground. The kids who excelled became the heroes.

Like many places where moral code is taught and practiced with rigidity and force, it also paradoxically attracted immorality… in this case, a pedophile.

Over the course of several years, the Shadow gained the trust of my parents and often visited our family home during the school year. At camp, he dealt me favorable hands and eventually convinced everyone it was a good idea for me to take trips with him.

And then, before I had experienced any sexual pleasure of my own, I was forcibly introduced to sexuality by this man in a cabin deep in the woods. Afterward, I could not tell the truth, so I placed my feelings into my shame basket and went on with life.

But years later, it was the work I conducted with this healer that allowed me to begin to have an empowered relationship with the experience.

In the beginning whilst working with her, I was relieved to have a reason as to why my life was such an apparent failure: why I had poor grades, struggled with my career and depression.

I believed I had been abused, tricked, fooled and betrayed.

But there was a huge part of me that was not satisfied with logic or reason. I knew I did not want to remain a victim of this experience. So, with the urging of my heart and the support of some close friends, I moved beyond rationalization and into feeling. I became aware of what felt like a psychic hole in my gut.

Never before had I ever felt anything like this. I began to notice this hole had a feeling associated with it, which was mostly dormant, but became activated in times of stress. Nevertheless, my shame basket was always in play.

It was like an open wound. It was a place inside of me that wasn't a part of my physical anatomy, but affected me physically.

This new association with an old part of myself allowed me to better understand some patterns of behavior I had been battling.

For years I had rapid cycles of weight gain and loss when I ate more food than my bodily hunger was asking for. There was also lust flowing in and out my life that didn't feel good to me. I kept it hidden through denial and shame.

Curious about this shame basket and deeply desiring to be whole, I immersed myself into the work I felt was necessary. I began to speak openly about my experiences and practiced forgiveness. I sought out healers and therapists. I wrote about my life and feelings, a lot.

For the first time, I decided that taking care of myself was the highest priority. I got really clear that I was going to open my heart and fall in love with myself.

I never imagined the implications of such audacity.

As soon as I began to come to terms with my shame basket and love myself more, everything I had been busily building in my life began to unravel – quickly.

The first, and most notable casualty was my marriage.

For 16 years, I had been the dutiful husband. I had gotten up for work 5-6 days a week. I keep the house together. I paid the bills. I did laundry. I coached soccer. I never strayed. What I did not know until later was, I wasn't really happy. Not even close.

There wasn't anything wrong with my marriage, or my family. Or anything.

I simply wasn't living my truth; an impossibility given the secret I had kept inside.

I had spent the last thirty years piling up experiences on top of not telling the truth about what happened with the Shadow and when that truth emerged, it was like pulling the foundation out from underneath a tall tower. Everything above collapsed into the empty space below.

EVERYTHING.

Leaving my marriage was the most difficult thing I have ever done. It surprised a lot of people. *I Never Saw It Coming*

It broke open the hearts of a lot of folks in my life. Many of them wouldn't speak to me for a long time. Some still don't.

I packed one suitcase and went to stay with a friend. It was the strangest and most heart-wrenching experience of my life. I knew I couldn't leave my family, and yet I absolutely had to follow through. I spent a lot of time in his guestroom trying to reconcile and make sense of what was happening.

Every night in my imagination, I held each of my children in my arms and spoke with them. I opened my heart and imagined my love could travel to them. It was powerful, and gave me a sense of hope.

Seven days into this new lifestyle, I was startled in the middle of the night by a tap on my shoulder and a voice that said:

"Awaken!"

I began to investigate my surroundings without getting up. Where am I? Again the voice said more loudly:

"Awaken!"

I sat upright in my bed and looked around.

The surroundings were unfamiliar to me, as I had not yet become accustomed to living away from home. My eyes focused on the dimly lit room. There was no one there. I reached for the bedside table.

My phone beamed 3:40am.

Suddenly I was stuck by a force that felt like the energy of a lightening bolt flowing through me with the force of a great waterfall.

I felt a great warmth and tingling sensation rising from the base of my spine, and my heart opened to an expanse of love. The energy was running through me and I felt connected to everything.

Holding the phone and feeling this energy, I was motionless, even though my entire body was shaking.

Intuitively, I recognized the energy running through me was textured with a language imbedded within its vibration. And as soon as I recognized the presence of this unfamiliar language, I somehow knew how to translate it into English.

This all happened in a moment… there was no time to reason. I could only feel and go with the flow. It became clear very quickly. This was not dialogue. This was about being receptive to a gift. It was a one-way communication. A transmission.

I typed the translation of the energy into the notepad of my phone with my two thumbs. It happened quickly. There was no time to correct misspellings or punctuate. Each new word came rapid fire. I was unable to intellectually process the information as I transcribed.

All of my attention was focused on staying completely present and getting the translation recorded.

After 90 minutes, the energy faded, as did the need to type. The faint light of daybreak came through my window. There was no more sleep for me. I lay back on the bed experiencing both sheer exhaustion and complete aliveness.

Vibrating from head to toe, I looked over the notes on my phone. The last line read:

Evolutionary Guideline One:

Allow Life To Come To You, And Act From Intuitive Feeling.

This was in direct opposition to how I had been living life for most of my 42 years. I had been chasing and trying to get what I thought I wanted, and it had just come tumbling down. Everything was gone.

EVERYTHING.

Except Your Now Open Heart.

Over the next 7 weeks, I received six more transmissions in a similar fashion in the wee hours of night. All typed with my thumbs on my phone.

Each one of these transmissions was another Evolutionary Guideline. They came in perfect order, and contained beautiful wisdom on how to shift personal consciousness to be more in harmony with one's heart, and for all people to become compassionate with one another.

It was a manual for catalyzing evolutionary change.

With the guidelines came a love affair with a beautiful soul. Together, we published a little green book:

The Evolutionary Guidebook – Follow Your Heart, BE Your Power

The Evolutionary Guidebook was my re-introduction to Sarza, and I carried it with me everywhere. One copy for reading, and others for giving as gifts to people I met.

In the beginning, everything in the book was new to me. I read it everyday, sometimes multiple times. My desire to integrate the material was strong. I began to teach classes and take on coaching clients to both share and absorb the guidelines.

I had fallen asleep as a small boy and awakened as a grown man.

I used to innocently fly with Sarza from my bed while my parents slept safely down the hallway. Now I wasn't innocent any longer. There were issues and people pulling at me from every direction. I had a pending divorce and a looming bankruptcy. Some tried to convince me I was mentally ill or in a mid-life crisis.

For most of my life I had cared too much about how people perceived me. Not anymore. I was relieved I didn't have to pretend to be someone else any longer.

New amazing things were happening. I could see stardust falling out of the sky during the day, and I was meeting extraordinary people to support my transition. I returned to traveling with Sarza into the galaxy at night and had found a new sense of peace.

Everything had become magical. I could feel a much broader matrix of consciousness and I could see how everything and everyone was connected. I could also see how the vast majority of people keep themselves blind to this truth.

The conventional world didn't make much sense to me any longer.

I had been *reFramed*.

As it turned out, the Shadow had given me a great gift. He had shown me a path to freedom. He gave me the location of my Shame Basket, and I had taken the courageous steps to open it and feel the truth of what I had pushed away for so long. This allowed me to get my SPAM up and burst through the layer of illusion that had kept me in the dark.

I could now see what was invisible to nearly everyone else.

And, I had a little green book to guide me.

What if you spoke
absolute truth all
the time?

What if you
came clean on
your secrets?

Would you shift into higher awareness?

Would a new truth emerge about life?

ReFrame Five

Power of Heart Language

How Do You Make Big Decisions?

It is uncomfortably hot.

The fool, now 16, sits outside slumped on a bench at summer camp. His energy is flat.

He feels idiotic and defeated. He is ashamed of his actions.

The maroon flame is burning within his abdomen, and yet a bright flame exists within his heart.

His head hangs and his eyes are averted from The Man.

I see the quiet confusion in The Man no one else does. "How has one of his top campers betrayed him like this?'

The fool has spent seven summers in a row at his camp - first as an enthusiastic youngster, then as decorated camp hero, and most recently as a less-than-inspired camp employee.

Inside, The Man's wife is speaking to the fool's father on the telephone. She is explaining why he must go home now. They are making flight arrangements.

While The Man watches, the fool takes the telephone. He would usually ask for his mother. He turns his back to hide his tears. I can see from my expanded awareness how ill his mother is, and how uncomfortable his father is in his newly expanded role of caregiver. He is doing the best he can.

The fool's soft crying tells his father he is on the line. He cannot speak. Suddenly the light within his heart expands, overtaking his sense of shame. The only words he can get out over his sudden sobbing to his father are: "*I Love You Dad.*"

He has never said this before, nor did he plan to say it. I watch as the light of his heart bridges the 400 miles of distance in an instant, allowing his father to receive the medicine of his words.

He is disarmed, and a battle is averted.

I want to tell the fool the power of what he has just said. I want to tell him that it was okay for him to get thrown out of camp to get away from the Shadow. I want to tell him now is the time to go home and tell his secret. I want to tell him he is always okay.

But despite my desire, my only influence is love now, and forgiveness later on.

By dinnertime he is at home. Within a few days, he begins a job digging ditches for new sewer lines in his neighborhood. His friends stop and watch him work on the way to the pool. It's the hottest summer in a decade.

He is not allowed to drive, see his friends socially, or leave the yard before he returns to a Christian boarding school in the fall.

As hard as the punishment is to swallow, anything is easier than having to face the Shadow everyday at camp... except, of course, telling his truth.

He is free, for now.

After the Evolutionary Guidebook was published, my partner and I had shared an incredible journey, all positive and absolutely transformative.

I began having a desire to move into a different living situation, which I hadn't communicated in fear of ending our relationship. My heart was overflowing with this desire despite not having any plans to do so, nor people to do it with. I simply wanted to live what was in the little green book.

But who was I to want something different than this? Why would I? Who in their right mind would give this up? Would she ask me to leave if she knew what I was feeling? Where would I go?

All I could do was be with my feelings and have the audacity to participate in some intimate truth telling. She must have sensed this was on the table, because she invited me to go out to dinner and have a very candid conversation. I imagined we would find a new place of honesty and things would continue as they had.

We went out to dinner and I let the truth fly… and she did the same. We gave each other the supreme gift of listening without knowing what would happen next. We stepped into allowance.

Within a couple of weeks, some acquaintances invited me for dinner at their large and gorgeous community home in the mountains. My partner was out of town. The Sky Temple was a place I had visited before.

It's a beautiful place on 35 acres in the mountains, and appropriately named. The entire home is extraordinarily decorated with altars to an emerging heart consciousness. There are gardens and thousands of pine trees surrounding the house.

The Sky Temple is a place to get your SPAM up.

Typically, there are 4-6 people living at Sky Temple at any given time. These are people who have dedicated their lives to being as spiritually conscious as possible, using the multiple reflections of community members to help them see their truth to evolve.

It is a place where spiritual aspirants and teachers alike gather for parties and meals to explore spiritual evolution. It is an ongoing experiment, a fascinating and enlightening place to spend time.

At the Sky Temple, play and laughter are valued at a very high level, as everyone who lives there is constantly reaching for the light. It is a unique way to live.

The bottom floor had been vacant for several months, and several times I had rejected their invitation for a number of logical and reasonable objections; including money, distance from my children and my current relationship status.

On this night however, things would shift. We were having a wonderful evening together. After dinner, while playing my guitar and singing with everyone in the living room, I felt my heart open. I spoke directly to my feeling.

> *"My heart is always open here!"*

Q, my friend whose wedding I would attend a year later in Hawaii, sensed an opportunity. He stopped everyone by holding up his arms. Waiting until the perfect moment of stillness and attention, he said:

> *"Then why do you keep saying 'No' to moving here?"*
>
> *Are you making this decision alone?*

The room remained quiet except for the beating of my heart. I felt naked. This was a new perspective that demanded nothing but the truth. As I felt into his questioning, the energy of my heart expanded and everything became serene and potent. There was only one choice.

"Okay, I'll do it!"

Surprised at how quickly my truth came out, I realized I had just ended my relationship. And while there was something scary about it all, it felt right.

The entire experience seemed to be oddly and magically self-organized without any effort on my part.

I had come to a *Choiceless Choice.*

Choiceless Choice

When the Truth You Feel is so Resonant with Your Soul, Resistance to Change is Futile.

Self-Directed Z-Energy.

Rapid Transformation.

Within a week, I moved into the sprawling home with plenty of room for my kids, and bawled my eyes out with my now-former partner as we sat in the mutual recognition of the ending of a chapter in both our lives.

The experience left me with a broken – open heart. It took me a while to recognize that my feelings of wanting to move were simply guiding me into my new truth, rather than being an indictment of my partner, our relationship or myself.

Living in community was the next step of my spiritual path that simply emerged after I spoke truthfully about my feelings. It was in alignment with the highest path for my life. It is what my heart desired, even though I did not consciously know it.

Communicating my authentic feelings with my former partner allowed the Choiceless Choice to present. I had been afraid to express my feelings, imagining I would create suffering for her, and lose what I needed in my life; namely support, shelter and partnership. I was in fear of the unknown.

This, of course, is a mind-oriented strategy to keep things the same. I was trying to control the outcome of my life by keeping my feelings under wraps.

But truthfully, I was holding both of us back, and as I would discover later, my children as well.

Not sharing these feelings was keeping my SPAM contracted and the relationship and myself from each respective potentiality.

Yes, it was me. Again.

End Act II

More Fool's Gold

The **Man** represents the authority to whom we give our power of discernment when we are unsure of life.

The **Shadow** represents aspects of ourselves we have chosen to ignore or hide. A human manifestation of our Shame Basket.

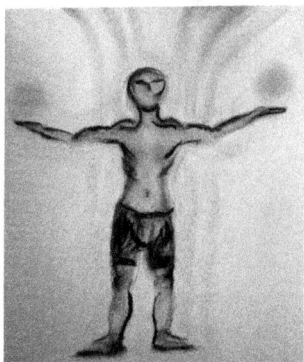

<u>Key to ReFraming is *to feel*</u>. If you feel it, you can heal it.

Use the SPAM Stance to convert hard emotions into heart feelings. This clears awareness and gets your SPAM up. *Do it now!*

<u>SPAM Stance Instructions:</u>

1) Find a grounded posture with a straight spine.

2) Take deep breaths into the belly, hold for 5 seconds.

3) Open your arms wide, lift your chin and expand the chest forward as much as possible. Stretch!

4) Keep breathing as deeply as possible with the intent to open your heart to feeling.

5) Ask for Divine help and visualize the streams of light-energy supporting you from Heaven and Earth.

Wouldn't your
truth attract
authentic people?

What if you
always spoke
from your heart?

Wouldn't
everyone else
run and hide?

How quickly would
you have a loving
community?

Sayulita, Mexico - Beach Labyrinth

Message from Sarza

All is Provided For Now

Dear Humans,

You have kept the lid so tightly on your shame, your hearts have been pinched into a kernel of pain.

This pain distorts perception and contributes to a layer of shame enveloping your planet. It hovers unseen near the ground like smog.

Were you to have vision, you would see your collective shame as maroon-colored, weaving like serpents and binding people at the navel.

You have become blind - tuning into drama, television and politics, instead of nature.

97

Why do you fear being alone with your feelings humans? Why do you reject them?

Instead you glorify competition to remain numb. You have become obsessed with who is winning.

But what is winning, if someone must always lose?

Be willing humans - to see how your repressed shame manifests as addiction, greed, obsession, disease, and ultimately as war.

Be willing humans - to see how the conditions you have placed on receiving what I have already given to you causes more suffering.

It doesn't have to be like this, dear humans. Shame cannot be maintained in a rising consciousness of love.

It is a simple solution: Raise your SPAM and teach others to do the same.

Ask the Medicine Children to show you how.

Medicine Children are shepherds to guide people into emotional, creative and spiritual freedom.

They are the seers. They are the explorers. Theirs is the language of nature.

They celebrate the great connectivity of all things and deeply yearn to remove the veils sophistication has placed over the hearts and minds of the people today.

They imagine. They play. They sing. They create. They know that every word, thought and deed affects the entire matrix of consciousness.

Their medicine challenges your status quo by stirring up still waters — to illuminate new ways of being for families, cities and societies.

Rather than take their medicine however, you force-feed them yours.

You belittle, project ridicule and coerce these beautiful beings into psychotropic medicines and institutions to keep them under control. You perceive they are too sensitive, weak and unimportant.

ReFrame dear humans, for they cannot hear you. It is you who must learn to listen to them.

These children (of all ages,) are to be revered. It is they who hold the key to humanity's collective empowerment.

I send more and more Medicine Children at this critical time in the evolution of human consciousness. We need them. You need them. I need them.

Otherwise I leave it to the natural Z-Energy forces of cause and effect to get your attention.

These Medicine Children are the Evolutionary Guides. They lead people through the heart passage to bring Sarza to Earth.

There is no shame in Sarza. There are no winners and no losers. The sick are healed, the children are happy. Everyone has a safe place to spend the night and good food to eat.

All is Provided For Now,

Sarza

Act III

ReFrame Six

The Value of One Peso

Who is Responsible for Your Emotional State?

The fool is now 39.

To his right sits a lawyer.   His left the seller.

Across sits a realtor.

He sits before a large stack of mortgage papers. A dream is coming true. His family gathers to celebrate outside the glass door. It's a day they have all been working toward.

Suddenly, something doesn't feel right in the fool's gut. It's a feeling he has never had before. He puts the pen down.

I can see the maroon flame begin to burn, hot.

Everyone is watching.

He takes a sip of water.

He is uncomfortable.

Sweat is forming on his brow. He feels trapped.

Only I see the perfection of the box he has created.

Watching him, I know he must push the first domino. It must be his choice alone. Perfection is at play, but only I can see it.

Little does the fool know the severity of the challenges just ahead. The economy will nearly collapse, his career will end and a major health challenge will befall his family, and they will lose their home. Then divorce.

He is hoping this is a good decision. However something doesn't feel right.

The fool has graduated from college, married, been successful in business, and won awards in sales. He is revered by friends and loved by family. He is an exceptional father. He is gifted.

But he does not know these things as truth yet.

Over the past few years, all intent and effort has gone toward this moment. Everything had lined up magically to be here now.

And yet suddenly, he has everyone's blessings but his own. He feels like a fool. What could be wrong with a home purchase for his family in the midst of a nice career acceleration?

As I watch him, I observe a brightening of his heart. The maroon flame in his gut also burns even brighter. There is anger.

From the outside all seems well in his world. On the inside, it is chaotic. Hasn't he been doing what he was supposed to be doing?

I watch as he considers walking away from the deal. I can see his mind imagine the pain and confusion around him. It would impact a lot of people.

Now the others in the room are suddenly nervous.

It feels like a huge moment for him. He needs more time. Everyone is watching.

I am humored. Only I know it matters not which path he takes from here, as both paths yield the exact same result. It doesn't matter which decision he makes. Eventually, the Dominos must fall. His soul's calling awaits.

I watch the energy of his heart shrink, and the maroon flames expand.

He has seen the joy in their eyes. He imagines the pain and suffering his truth will cause.

He pushes the feeling down into his abdomen, placing a few more Dominos onto an already teetering network of play pieces. He takes a big breath and begins signing papers...

Just after moving into Sky Temple I was in Mexico.

Afterward, I found myself standing on the crowded bus to the Puerto Vallarta airport reading the novel, *Siddhartha*. It was the first book I had read in nearly five years.

Siddhartha is about a man in the time of Buddha who renounces his material possessions and sets out on a journey with a begging bowl with the intent of reaching enlightenment.

The book details an extraordinary journey of giving everything away, surrendering to the moment and experiencing extraordinary grace, adventure and lessons along the way.

Curiously, the word *Siddhartha* is made up of two words in the Sanskrit language, *siddha* (achieved) + *artha* (meaning wealth) which together mean "he who has found meaning of existence."

Whether it was my complete immersion in the book, the letting down of my guard because I was at the end of a big week of adventure, or more likely, the deep spiritual desire to really know the true meaning of "*All is Provided for Now*," I apparently became an easy target for a pickpocket who relieved me of my wallet and passport sometime during the bus trip.

It wasn't until I arrived at the airport later in the day that I discovered my wallet and passport were missing. Remembering the bump from someone on the bus, it wasn't difficult to put the pieces together.

Here I was... traveling alone in a large foreign city, late in the day, without any money or identification, unfamiliar with the language at the beginning of a weekend.

I Never Saw it Coming!

After a few moments of anger and a loud expletive, I surrendered. I was being presented with an amazing opportunity.

I had called this challenge to me, and now it was time to find the gift. I simply needed an immediate link-up to a higher state of awareness.

I took a moment to enter the *power paradox*, accepting 100% responsibility for creating this situation without needing to control it.

I assumed the SPAM Stance.

I paused with the busyness of the airport travelers swirling all around, set down my bags, looked to the sky, raised my gaze, spread my arms, took a big breath into my belly, opened my heart to my feelings and asked for help.

Holding this posture as long as I could, I stretched open my chest and took several more deep breaths into my belly and heart. I allowed whatever feelings were present to expand in my chest beyond my body.

While imagining having the support of Father Sky and Mother Earth, I visualized energy rising within me and descending upon me to expand my heart and declared "I AM returning home safety."

The opening of my heart must have made a connection to something beyond my previous awareness because for the next six days I experienced an amazing flow of serendipity.

I knew that partnership was important in this moment despite traveling alone, and I began to look for ways to be in harmony with the people around me.

Moments later, a caring 19-year old bilingual local man stopped me as I tried to board a bus without any money. He listened to my situation and became my guide for the next hour, helping me get in touch with the proper authorities and paying for my bus fare to the terminal to report the theft.

Together, we learned the US Consulate was closed until Tuesday for a Mexican holiday. I had three nights before I could begin to get a new passport.

With nothing else he could do for me, my gracious benefactor gave me the gift of 50 pesos so I could buy a street taco and take the bus back to the town where I had spent the last week on retreat.

When I arrived, it was 7:45pm and dark.

Finding a café to use the wireless connection, I checked my bank balance and discovered I had been double charged earlier for a gift I had purchased in town, right down the street.

I immediately walked to the store and was refunded the money in cash just as they were closing.

I then ran into someone who I had met earlier in the week on the beach. Before I had said a word about my situation, he extended an invitation to have dinner with his family in a local restaurant and afterwards gave me a ride to the neighborhood where I had stayed.

Knocking on the door of the person who rented me the accommodations and explaining my circumstance, I was graciously provided a complimentary stay in a 1-bedroom casita for as long as I needed it.

The entire day seemed to be oddly and magically self-organized without any effort on my part.

Within hours of my passport and wallet being stolen, I had a nice place to stay, a full belly, a few days worth of groceries and money in my pocket. And with no way of getting a new passport until Tuesday, I began a personal vision quest.

For the next three days I did what I felt like doing. I walked alone up and down empty beaches, exploring the jungle and the inner landscape of my consciousness.

On Tuesday, I left the jungle casita on foot to catch the same bus to Puerto Vallarta on which I had been pickpocketed.

I was going to visit the US Consulate and noticed that I was leaving the comforts of the little village I knew well, heading again into the unknowns of a foreign city. About half of the money remained and I was feeling certain everything would work itself out perfectly.

When I arrived at the US Consulate office, I was enveloped by the stories of the other Americans standing in line who had been victimized and inconvenienced by pickpockets and/or thieves. It was like they were all trying to win a story-telling contest.

They told their stories a second time to the people working behind the bulletproof glass when it was their turn to apply for their new passports. They spoke loudly to be heard through the small opening and ignorantly to the relevance of their tale to their host.

I watched the entire scene with a great deal of curiosity and humor, and when it was my turn I simply filled out the form and sat down, only sharing the parts of the story which were necessary.

The process required all American citizens to first fill out the paperwork and then wait for a meeting with the Chief Consulate, who after confirming your identity and your predicament administered an oath as testament to American citizenship.

When it was my turn, the Chief Consulate asked me a few questions about my situation and told me I would receive a replacement passport via UPS in two to three days time.

"Do you have a place to stay?" she asked. After hearing my response, she said she would arrange something for me and asked me to wait.

As the guards were closing the office for the day at 12:30 p.m. the Chief Consulate reappeared and walked me out of the office over to a gorgeous resort down the street.

Impeccably landscaped grounds complete with swimming pools and fountains met my eyes as we entered the gates. As we walked past the guard and headed down an open hallway, she took a key chain off her wrist and said to me:

"There is something about you that tells me you will be good on your word. I am offering this condominium, use of the swimming pool and whatever food and drink is available inside, until you receive word your passport is ready, under the agreement you will pay a fee of $100 to the owner at some point in the future. Here is the address in the States to send the money. Don't change your airline ticket until you know your passport is ready to be picked up. Leave the key on the counter."

With that she opened the door to a beautifully decorated 3-bedroom condominium whose porch looked out onto the marina, quickly showed me around, handed me the key and said goodbye.

And so, for the next two days I walked up and down the busy coastline awaiting word about my passport. I was deeply curious about the contrasts of life, and how a man with barely $20 to his name could be surrounded by and enjoy such abundance.

On the second afternoon, word came via email that my passport would be ready in the morning. By this time, I had eaten all the food in the condominium and had very little money left, mostly change.

I decided to take one more walk down the beach. It was a gorgeous day and people were enjoying the warmth and the ocean. I found a quiet place to journal and meditate when a very strong feeling opened inside my heart. I clearly heard the following:

Care Less About Acquiring Money.

Learn to live in total abundance with what naturally comes to you through inspiration and service.

It was at this moment, I began to truly recognize the significance of my life's journey.

For years, I had been inspired to spiritually counsel people on a donation-only basis. If they couldn't pay, I'd serve them anyway. I kept saying *yes* to serving.

It was always an interesting challenge for me operating a donation-based practice inside the linear economic framework of America while raising three children. Everyone else was doing it differently, but I was now seeing how beautifully it allowed me to live right on the edge and evolve. I was simply in sync with my soul's blueprint.

I had been learning how to receive what was offered, period. There were no rules, only a little green book and Sarza's promise that *All is Provided For Now*.

This left me without the customary funds to operate my life on occasion. There was one constant, however. When I opened my heart, what I needed always showed up. I was learning to flow in the currency of love.

The Currency of Love

A Perfect Flow of Resources Presenting from Infinite Channels When SPAM is Up.

Evolutionary Abundance.

This time alone in Mexico had given me an expanded perspective. I could see how the constant mindset of trying to acquire money had kept me from my heart.

For most of my life, I had tried to 'fix the money problem' repeatedly by taking a multitude of self-help workshops and programs. I had tirelessly worked with coaches, affirmations and even hypnotherapy. But, I kept coming back to the same place of futility. The perspective of hindsight revealed how I was missing the gifts hidden amongst my financial challenges my soul wanted me to receive.

Trying to fix the problem only created more suffering.

I was beginning to see the truth our larger culture conceals so well - Everyone has a "money issue" they try and fix to avoid suffering. Paradoxically, this keeps them stuck in conditional receptivity; conditional love, conditional abundance and condition acceptance.

Now, I could see that by losing the condition, I could also lose the 'problem.'

All I ever had to do was to go into the emotion of shame surrounding my perceived limitations, feel them deeply with appreciation and then let go into the heart.

I could use the SPAM Stance to raise my SPAM — which opened new channels of receiving to naturally shift my experience.

Sarza was always showing me how to flow in the Currency of Love: Open my heart, reFrame and trust that *All is Provided For Now*.

I finally saw how my financial challenges had been an incredible teacher of self-compassion, allowing me to receive exactly what I needed, rather what I thought I needed. Or what other people wanted me to need.

In doing so, I could quickly move into gratitude for the perfection of life, and enjoy what was present. I could be free in a way I have never imagined before.

Looking up from my meditation on the beach, I noticed the sun setting over the water and could feel my time in Mexico drawing to a close. I walked back to the condominium in the glow of the setting sun and put my things together for the journey home.

The next morning I awoke, showered and put on my backpack, left the condominium key on the counter as requested and plodded down to the bus stop.

Several hours later, after retrieving my passport from the UPS office and hungry for my first meal of the day, I emptied my pockets for the remaining money.

81 pesos.

Running late, I ran down to the main thoroughfare and hailed the first cab I saw. *How many pesos to the airport?* I asked in really bad Spanish.

"Eighty Pesos senor!" was the answer.

I piled in, giving him the fare and tucking the one peso remaining in my pocket for good luck.

When I finally had my ticket and was headed to the gate on the escalator, I began to cry from a place of gratitude, exhaustion and the sudden realization how fortunate I had been to be pickpocketed. I had received an extraordinary gift.

The entire experience seemed to be oddly and magically self-organized without any effort on my part.

I amusingly wondered if Sarza had orchestrated it all by sending a secret agent disguised as a thief.

Completely cracked open and red-faced, I walked into a fast food shop and asked the first person I saw to buy me a meal.

Eating an amazing fish sandwich and fingering the one peso, I texted my housemate: "*All Has Been Provided For...* boarding *Now.*

See you at the airport in Denver."

What if you
focused on serving
from passion?

What if you
stopped fixing
your money?

Would you have
more fun and get
your SPAM up?

Wouldn't you
receive what you
need and more?

ReFrame Seven

Activate Adventures in Nature

Are You Complete With Old Relationships?

The fool is 45.

His life dreams seem elusive. He feels alone.

He cannot seem to break all the way through and keep his SPAM up to share his gifts authentically.

After college graduation, he went on a month-long backpacking adventure in California to hike the John Muir Trail. It was his first trip to the West Coast of the United States.

The giant Sequoia and Redwood trees of Muir Woods were of particular interest to him during the trip. He found it curious how much he suddenly appreciated trees.

Caught in an early snowstorm on the last days of the trip and unable to finish, he would carry the memory of 'not-finishing' for 23 years.

Each year, the fool makes a promise to himself to finish, awaiting the perfect time or measure of success to justify time and expense. Finally at 45 years of age, he decides to make a run for California. To finance the trip, he gives up his apartment for the deposit money and couch-surfs for a while. He has enough cash and food to get to California and hike, but not enough for the return trip.

The day before he leaves, doubts creep into his mind, and he decides to hike in Colorado instead to save the gas money. He goes by a friend's house to borrow supplies. While he is waiting for his friend to retrieve the items, he sees a poster on the wall, and is entranced by its message:

NEVER GIVE UP

"No matter what is going on
Never give up
Develop the heart
Too much energy in your country
Is spent developing the mind
Instead of the heart
Be compassionate
Not just to your friends
But to everyone
Be compassionate
Work for peace
In your heart and in the world
Work for peace
And I say again
Never give up
No matter what is going on around you
Never give up"

His Holiness, the Dalai Lama XIV

The next morning the Fool leaves for California. Before he does, he gets clear on his intent. He stands in SPAM Stance and declares: "I AM finishing the trail and returning home safety."

It's an epic adventure.

On the way, he calls Minnie, explaining how he is heading out to finish the trail he nearly completed after college. Minnie, of course, remembers it all perfectly. She had done what any mother would have done. She talked to Jesus about keeping her white son safe out there in the woods, and never said a word about worrying about the bears. She helped him organize the food and supplies he would need for the journey.

She talked to his white Momma in Heaven and told her she was doing the best she could. After all, she had survived breast cancer, while his birth Momma had not.

When Minnie retired from the family after 30 years, she was given a paid vacation as a retirement gift. She could have gone anywhere, but she chose to go to Colorado and visit the Fool and his family.

He is Her Son indeed.

On this day, she is sending off more prayers and handing out unsolicited advice – which the Fool always likes to receive. These calls are precious.

"It's yo job to love you," she says. "Ain't nobody gonna do it for you – no how – no way."

That night he sleeps in the car after driving 16 hours straight. And by the afternoon the following day, he is hiking.

It's a 50-mile solo journey into the wilderness. He hikes quickly, but completely aware. He uses his power, but surrenders to nature. He hears hardly a sound, but listens to the trees in a new way. He climbs Mt Whitney, and from a place higher than any point in California, the Fool hears:

> *Stop teaching and start living. Trust and surrender completely to the Heart.*

Walking down the mountain, he is ecstatic about finishing the journey 23 years later. His SPAM is way up, and he sets his intent on making it back to Colorado safely and easefully. At the end of the trail, a man stands waiting. He asks, "Where are you headed? I have money for gas."

It's not quite in the direction he needs to go, but The Fool is on board – "Let's go," he says. And a new adventure begins.

One day later after dropping off the hitchhiker, he is near the Arizona / Nevada border still needing gas money. He passes a sign:

> *Last Exit for Casino.*

Moments later a car passes him going the opposite direction. The license plate reflects his headlights with a beam of light back to him he cannot ignore. It's a gold vanity plate that says:

BLK-11.

Taking it as a sign, the Fool checks his mirror and turns hard right to catch the exit at the last possible moment. He pulls into the hotel, and walks into the casino. He scans the great room with his awareness in appreciation of the music, the sounds and the lights. There is magic in the air. He can feel the power of the moment.

His SPAM is up.

One roulette table seems brighter than the others. The dealer stands ready. There is no one else at the table. The Fool sits down, and looks at the dealer with a great deal of curiosity. The dealer is beaming and sporting an impeccable uniform, flawless hair, and an extraordinary smile. He turns away to spin the roulette wheel. He slowly turns back the Fool: **You Gotta Get Your Bet Up!**

The Fool quickly places one of his coveted twenty-dollar bills on *BLK-11*. Everything slows down as I watch the space around the table conform to the power of his intent. The game piece is skipping slowly across the spinning circular board.

The Fool can see the slot of *BLK-11* shining brightly, as though energized. The ball bounces high and arcs through the air with great precision.

He has been dealt a favorable hand.

The ball lands on *BLK-11* and sticks into the slot like a puzzle piece. The dealer smiles, turns and begins to count chips.

The Pit Boss comes over. The Man is a towering figure, like a skyscraper. He watches the dealer push $680 in chips across the table with a scowling look, and whispers something into his ear of his deputy.

Only a fool would try his luck again. He flips the dealer $20, and places another $20 bet on BLK-11 - then another, and another.

Suddenly, the fool's energy contracts to match his surroundings. He feels the energy around him dive. He notices just how lifeless a casino can be, while I see a stream of faint maroon smoke winding its way through the great room like a giant snake.

The dealer suddenly seems to be on life support. The Fool notices that his skin is grey. He is unkempt, slightly overweight and has scraggly sideburns. His posture is slouched.

There is something about this man that repulses the Fool and invites the fool to stay longer. The dealer gives him a funny look, saying:

Oh, I've seen a lot people come through here my friend —
you ain't any different than the rest of them.

Sarza is speaking through the Shadow. The Fool walks away from the table and heads for the parking lot. I watch him drive into the night, listening to the wind whistle through the open sunroof. Occasionally he looks to see if the moon is still following him home.

The entire day seemed to be oddly and magically self-organized without any effort at all.

I know he is curious about how he is going to get by without teaching for it is his main source of income. I can also see how he is beginning to truly appreciate his persistence and resolve to see things through.

I see a man who never gives up, and who never settles for anything less than the truth. But I see a man who needs more support for his transition period to be complete.

Only I know how much he will require an entire community to assist him through the next part of the journey.

The Sky Temple will embrace him soon.

When he arrives back in Colorado, I watch as he meets a woman at a party. She is beaming, impeccably dressed with flawless hair. She has an extraordinary smile.

Over the course of a few months, she gains the
trust of the fool and often visits his home,
unannounced. She eventually convinces him that it
is a good idea to take trips with her in her new
maroon automobile.

Living in community at the Sky Temple is far more
than simply living with friends. It's an ongoing recipe-
from-scratch for accelerated growth and Z-energy.
You can never tell how, when or from where the next
great lesson will plow into your life.

Sometimes you can go months without being
challenged and then suddenly you don't want to come
out of your room for fear of facing the darkest parts of
your being. One thing is for certain. There is no way to
keep personal aspects hidden. Co-habituating with
people dedicated to living a conscious life brings
forward those elements ready to be transformed.

Sometimes the reFrame is easeful and immediate,
happening in the kitchen over dinner or coffee. And
occasionally, more extreme methods are needed.

Our community revolves around a large common
room with a vaulted ceiling and huge windows
overlooking the forest, with the lights of Boulder in the
distance.

We call it the *Temple Room*. It's where we gather for everything. Extraordinary teachers, musicians, artists, shamans and priestesses of every kind have graced our Temple Room. Surrounded by deities, alters, candles, sacred geometrical art, and heart rocks, the community gathers here a few times a month for check-ins, reflection and intention setting.

We believe deeply in the power of the group harmonic field surrounding us as a link to Divine intelligence, and are diligent about keeping the space energetically consistent with our intent.

Often we gather in a ReFrame Circle in the Temple Room. When we come together, we open with prayer and sit in a circle with the mission to get our SPAM up and find the gifts within our challenges.

We let Sarza guide us all the way. We have found when we really surrender to the circle and listen deeply through our hearts, solutions present themselves we couldn't see before.

For instance, new roommates appear and old ones leave in perfect synchronicity with the energy, as long as we stay connected and in allowance.

When someone wants to accomplish something specific or has a request for assistance with their spiritual growth, the community gathers to empower them.

We help them flush out old emotions, find their heart's true desire and then set a clear intention.

From a place of clarity, we collectively amplify the frequency of their intention by feeling it as already manifested in each of our hearts. In special cases, we gather to resolve tension that affects the collective SPAM of the household.

Just before starting to write ReFrame, it was my turn to be challenged in this way. My challenges were a detriment to the community. I had unresolved issues with two community members reflecting in the forms of my archetypal friends: The Man and the Shadow.

The Man was present to teach me to stand in and speak my truth, and then to follow through with my heart's desires with or without his approval.

This was something I never felt completely comfortable doing in my life, and I had been carrying the burden for too long.

The Shadow was present to help me learn the power of being clear with boundaries, and completely trusting my intuition to take better care of myself on all levels.

Both situations arose at the same time. Quickly, my SPAM was low and drama was in the house. It seemed like no matter how I attempted to bring these relationships back into balance, the drama remained.

I knew I was 100% responsible for attracting and perpetuating both situations, and the resolution would come from shutting my mouth and surrendering to the heart. It was my turn to take the medicine from the community by practicing deep listening.

Deep Listening

Listening Innocently With Your Heart, Allowing All Feeling to Freely Flow.

Radical Self-Responsibility.

In the first situation, The Man and I agreed to deep listening with the entire community. Five people sat together in this space to create a sacred container for transformation.

Within a few hours, The Man and I both entered a new place of understanding when our minds let go of the old story and our hearts opened to one another. Both of us felt something new, powerful and transformative.

We experienced an immediate spiraling up of awareness as tears flowed.

The reFrame became clear. A shift occurred.

A gift appeared. Forgiveness was immediate.

We got our SPAM up.

But in the other situation, regardless of how many times we sat together, with and without community support, drama remained. Deep listening was not possible. Instead we were practicing *drama looping*.

Drama Looping

Any Participation in the Transference of Shame Between People.

Blame. Self Sabotage. Dream Stealing.

Enslaved by Conditional Joy.

My only recourse was to get simple, really simple. I went to spend time deep listening in nature, alone.

This time I didn't have to drive to California. I simply walked outside. I went hiking in the woods around Sky Temple, paying close attention to all movement, patterns, colors and animal life.

From a place of deep desire to know the truth, I asked the trees for their wisdom. I hugged them to feel their vertical energy running from and into the Earth and the sky, and visualized my SPAM like theirs.

I told the trees about my challenges. I asked for their assistance. Listening for the answers, I heard:

I AM Sarza, the self-organizing field.

I keep everything in perfect order… the forests, the stars, the planets and the galaxies.

When you connect to Me, your life easefully falls into natural order because I AM Divine perfection.

Go now and carve new pathways.

I immediately went to the garage to get shovels and a pickaxe with the intent of converting the tension of my trials to create new trails. I began to walk around the acreage of the Sky Temple imagining people hiking to beautiful meditation spots.

I looked at the land and the rocks. I hiked up and down the existing animal trails. When I started to sense a pattern, I began carving new pathways into the land, imagining I was cutting new flows of thought and feeling into my personal consciousness as well.

I made the trails both artistic and functional, following the rhythms of the land and listening for how they would like to twist through the trees. I chose to have fun and surrender to the project, becoming the trails themselves.

Anytime I discovered my mind engaged in the drama of the relationship entanglement with the Shadow, I assumed the SPAM Stance to shift the old emotion into love. When I felt anger or frustration, I took to the pickaxe or moving rocks.

Days later, I returned to my life with new clarity.

The drama was still present in the relationship. Deep listening had become impossible. We could no longer hear one another. We had different truths.

As difficult as it was, it was evident my truth was taking me away from her. It was time to separate. Our SPAM simply did not match any longer.

It wasn't personal, never was and never will be.

My regret would come later… for in the end, I left the door to the relationship slightly ajar.

Would you be
able to hear
new things?

What if you
committed to
deep listening?

Wouldn't you become more attractive?

Would that bring success in love and in life?

ReFrame Eight

Evolutionary Forgiveness

How Do We Return To Innocence?

The fool is 46.

He is in his hometown for a family reunion.

The kids are in bed, and a friend has picked him up to take him to a party they cannot find.

They are in an unfamiliar side of town. It's late. The fool is slightly annoyed. Giving up on their plans, they pull into a music joint.

In the sparse audience is a man he met years ago. He is a Musician who resonates with all people. Over a beer, the Fool feels empowered to share a personal vision. Despite how ridiculous it sounds in his mind, he shares anyway.

"I've been singing ***The Ho'Oponopono Prayer*** for the past few years, and I've noticed incredible changes happening in my life."

> *I AM Sorry*
> *Please Forgive Me*
> *I Love You*
> *Thank You*

The Fool goes on to describe accounts of miraculous healing which have occurred in people purely from recitation of the prayer. In fact, people have been healed simply from other's recitation, while in ignorance of the prayer's use.

"I am curious," he says. What would happen if millions of people began singing along with songs of forgiveness? Could we shift the collective consciousness with popular music?"

The Musician is no fool. He is moved by the vision.

Two weeks later, an inspired Fool arrives back in Nashville and walks into a recording studio. There sits the Musician plus eight others with instruments in hand. They are all eager to give freely to the project. They are inspired.

By the end of the night, a song has come into focus. After two more studio sessions in Nashville over the summer, a song of forgiveness is produced. He sings the song hundreds of times over the course of the project, as do his new friends.

The entire experience seemed to be oddly and magically self-organized without any effort at all.

Later in the fall, a short music documentary about the song is created and shown at a film festival in Nashville. It is called *Pono Pono*. It is a great honor for the Fool, and he is inspired to make more art; specifically resonant art that inspires awakening.

But something is bothering him.

The project didn't quite have the impact he hoped it might. He imagined the project to have had a different level of success.

> *In due time my foolish Fool... patience. There is more*
> *clearing to be done.*

Instead, the project revealed another Shadow.

One of the band members severely challenged the fool and exhibited the need for control over the project. I see a truth he cannot see yet.

This project was simply an intermediate step. It was an opportunity to practice compassion within first.

I do see a man however, who had the courage to follow the inspiration of his heart, all the way back to his hometown – to forgive. He has spent more time in the last 6 months in Nashville since he moved away 25 years ago. I see a man becoming at peace with his past.

While in town for the film festival, he spends the night in his childhood room at his family home by himself. Something feels different – I sense it. A desire is building. He is restless and cannot sleep. Late at night the Fool is awake. He gets out of bed and stands in the bright moonlight shining through the window. To his left is the garage.

Looking out over the garden designed by his mother 40 years ago and beautifully maintained by his father since her death for the last 25, he finds new love for Colonial Hall and his heritage.

He opens his stance, and lifts his heart to the heavens. He feels deeply the appreciation of his Father. He sees just how perfect his life journey has been. Everything he has experienced has been perfectly perfect. He has received everything he needed to be here - right now.

EVERYTHING.

I watch what he cannot see. A brilliant cord of light is arcing from behind the moon. It drops from the sky and anchors in his heart. Transformation is happening at a level only seen beyond the bounds of time and space.

I whisper in his ear:

> *Keep singing, playing and following your heart. Go into nature and carve new pathways.*

Meanwhile on this same night, an unknown woman kneels in the sand of a Florida beach.

The white crystals are reflecting the moon as they absorb her tears. Her journey has been a challenging one.

She left her birthplace of Australia but hasn't found a new place to call home. Her heart is opening to something new. She desires to be free.

She looks to the heavens and spreads her arms wide, sending her intent for true love into the *Eternal* space above. She imagines having someone in her life that is authentic, and encourages her to be fully empowered. She imagines him to be amazing and free. She imagines they will make beautiful art together.

She is perfect.

One day I was shipping the final version of "Pono Pono" (a short forgiveness film) to the Artlightenment Film Festival in Nashville.

I had just placed the DVD into the shipping package and while filling out the address slip. I noticed a woman next to me doing the same thing.

It was a woman who had confided in me three years before about some challenges she was having in relationship with her child and a sibling.

I reintroduced myself. Within minutes, she explained she was recovering from breast cancer, and that she was beating it. I became very curious at this point, and inquired whether her family issues had resolved.

She told me she was in a bitter lawsuit with her sibling and hadn't spoken to her child since the recent birth of her grandchild.

Curious about the serendipity of dropping a forgiveness film into the mail while this woman was sending legal documents, I suggested, "Perhaps you could practice forgiveness with them."

"Oh no," she replied sharply, "It's not about me. I have done nothing wrong." And she went on to great length to explain all the reasons why she wasn't at fault and why forgiveness would not work. "Besides," she said. "My spiritual community has taught me, *there is nothing to forgive*."

Recognizing the end of conversation, I said goodbye.

I did however retain a great deal of curiosity about our interaction. It was intense. Her resolute position on forgiveness was fascinating, as she appeared to be in terrific emotional pain. Of all the things she said, it was the final statement that had the most energy.

> *"There is nothing to forgive."*

When words hang around in my consciousness, I have learned they have medicine for me.

Within a few weeks I was back in Mexico one year after the One Peso story. This year I was choosing to spend six weeks in the jungle near the beach. Publically, I was preparing to facilitate a Vision Quest and writing my book, ReFrame. Privately, I was there to clear the shame that kept attracting shadows.

I could feel I wouldn't be the same man when I returned to the States – and while one part of me was absolutely thrilled for this, one part was scared, really scared.

I knew another part of me had to die, again.

I spent the first week alone in spiritual practice, walking through the jungle, and writing. I was clear on my intent to empty my shame basket. I utilized the SPAM Stance every day.

One day while on the beach, I heard:

> *Be curious about the journey beyond forgiveness.*
>
> *What happens when you observe a difficult situation from multiple perspectives?*
>
> *Could you see your way out of the hedge maze?*

While in Mexico, 24 people would come to visit including my children, friends, and Vision Quest clients. It turned out to be the perfect way to explore multiple perspectives.

We made no plans, and simply set intentions as guided by our hearts. Everyone agreed to enter a space of transparency by practicing Deep Listening and telling the truth of their feelings.

We focused on celebrating life and let Sarza handle the details of what we needed to learn.

In this evolutionary space, everyone became the voice of Sarza's wisdom. And everyone who had the courage to listen to the voice of multiple perspectives made rapid evolutionary leaps.

I was no exception.

Multiple Perspectives

*The Conscious Choice to Notice **Everyone** has Evolutionary Medicine for Your Journey.*

Listening for Sarza's Wisdom as People Speak And Respond to Your Character.

Over my time in Mexico, it was extraordinary what I learned about myself – especially when I became clear nothing coming out of anyone's mouth was personal. It was merely data for my spiritual journey.

I simply had fun, spoke from the heart, listened deeply, and was incredibly inquisitive about all interactions with people.

In the middle of the trip, I found myself locked out of the house I had rented.

Curiously, the hand bolt inside the door locked while the house was empty, and I had no way back inside. The keys were useless.

Earlier, I had made sure the windows were locked because my children had just arrived. I was sure the only way into the house was to break in. After a loud expletive and a few minutes spent fumbling with the door, I stepped away and assumed the SPAM Stance. Immediately I was in touch with Sarza, and was surprised at what I heard.

> *If you want to get back into the house, make a deal with Me.*

"I didn't know I could make a deal with You."

> *Do you want the deal or not?*

"I want to get back in the house… okay, yes! What do I have to do?"

> *Pull in your lust. Following lust invites Shadows and all human suffering.*
>
> *Instead, focus on your heart's desire. Open to your truest desire and receive.*
>
> *Do this well, and you can write the book you truly desire to pen.*

Wow, Sarza wasn't fooling around.

Moments later, my middle daughter walked around the corner of the house. I asked her to see if the back door somehow got left open. We walked around the house together to check. It was locked from the inside.

On the way back, we passed the locked window of the kitchen. I was inspired to check it anyway.

It opened.

I smiled and looked to the Heavens.

Recognizing the futility of knowing whether the window was really unlocked or not beforehand, I went on with my day.

A deal had been made.

It was now time to live it.

The next few days were a great challenge. It was hot everywhere, especially on the beach. It seemed like I was being purposefully challenged as everywhere I turned, there was something trying to ignite my lust.

Women were suddenly contacting me out of the blue over email and text, and my mind was constantly reminding me of old habits.

I kept things really simple by pouring my energy into my art, and using the SPAM stance to clear the shame energy from my body and keep my heart open.

Every time I noticed myself becoming interested in following the lust, I would transfer my intent to face my shame instead. This was a powerful internal action as it shone the light of clarity on the truth behind the feeling.

By placing myself in SPAM Stance and opening my heart, I found I could expand the lust into a lighter and freer energy of love. From this place of deep feeling, I recited the Ho'Oponopono Prayer repeatedly.

> *I AM Sorry*
> *Please Forgive Me*
> *I Love You*
> *Thank You*

Some days I would recite the prayer for hours on the beach, or sing it walking through the jungle. I was speaking the prayer to the feeling of shame itself.

Anytime a story presented itself to me, I would skip the dramatic features and go right back to forgive the feeling. It took vigilance and practice.

Five days later the pain of my shame basket became more noticeable. I started shaking. I knew intuitively what was happening. I spent a good deal of the next few hours in the bathroom as my body physically ejected the shame stored within it.

I felt much better immediately. My SPAM was way up.

Soon after, I was unexpectedly given a didgeridoo by a friend on the beach. The didgeridoo is the ancient instrument of the Aboriginal people of Australia. It is an instrument I love to play, but I had left mine back in the States. Anytime I play, I feel my heart open.

For the days leading up to the Vision Quest, I played it every day. One afternoon on the beach, its true magic was revealed to me while playing for some friends.

I became aware of the power of embedding my intent into the sounds I was making. I could even see the geometrical shapes of the sounds leaving the instrument. I began infusing prayer into the music to send transmissions into the *Evermore*.

For the rest of the day, I had the best time transmitting sound prayers. Toward the end of the day, I decided to create one of my own. Having honored the deal with Sarza, the heartfelt desire for a sacred union romantic partner blossomed. I found a place on the beach that felt right.

Digging my feet into the sand, I opened up my arms, lifted my chin and asked for help.

I went into SPAM Stance to imagine a relationship in which both lives are uplifted by one another. I imagined having someone in my life that is authentic, and encourages me to be fully empowered. I imagined her to be amazing and free. I imagined we would make beautiful art together. I imagined she would love my children, and they, her.

I began to play the didgeridoo, calling her in.

It is the morning of a perfect day.

The Fool sits on the porch of a casa in Mexico. He is awaiting ten participants for the Vision Quest who are due to arrive in the afternoon.

His newly–acquired didgeridoo leans next to him against the bench.

He is taking these last few hours of free time to continue writing his new book, imagining how he can answer the call to share his gifts to help shift the collective consciousness. He is a Fool indeed.

A car pulls up in the driveway. There is commotion and the sound of a rolling suitcase; a guest is arriving early.

Embarrassment sweeps over him, as he, expecting no one until later, has neither cleaned himself nor the house. He is unprepared for what is happening and only I can see just how fortunate he is.

Seconds later, a woman is on the porch with him.

She explains she has come to drop her friend off for the Vision Quest, only to stay a moment or two.

She is older than he. A beautiful conversation ensues. She wants to know about his children and how he came to be in Mexico leading the Quest. How has he come to his life's work? She is a wonderful listener.

He tells her more than he normally would to just anyone. They spend much more time together than planned. At the end of the conversation, the Fool offers her a copy of *The Evolutionary Guidebook*.

She accepts.

Opening the book for the inscription, he says to the woman: "Excuse me, but if we exchanged names, I have forgotten yours."

"We didn't exchange names," she says. "Make it out to Judith **Ray**. You can call me Judy."

There is a long silence while a stunned Fool looks into Judy's eyes, and awkwardly says, "My name is E, E. Dan Smith."

Almost as if looking for a hint of recognition, he says, "I come from Nashville, Tennessee."

Another moment passes. Judy says nothing, except a smile.

He signs the names slowly, purposefully. Handing the book back to her, he asks: "May I ask you a favor? It might be strange to you."

"Anything." says the woman.

"My mother's name was Judith **Gray**. She died a long time ago, before I could really say goodbye. I feel like I never really knew her – or her me. Throughout this trip, I have felt her presence and now I am feeling this moment to be a Divine opportunity – a gift from God."

"I'd like to embrace you."

Judith **Ray** opens her arms to the Fool.

He melts into the embrace and feels deep love for his momma - allowing himself the nurturing which can only come from the Great Mother.

Neither of them can see the cord of light coming out of the Earth up through the slots of the wooden porch. It embraces him from below. I see his heart expand.

He smiles.

Judy smiles too.

The tears would come later.

On the sixth day of the Vision Quest, a forgiveness labyrinth was created in the beach sand at low tide.

We held the collective intent of opening to the power of forgiveness without knowing exactly how it would work. We created a beautiful altar in the center so the incoming tide would take our prayers into the ocean. We decorated the labyrinth and prepared ceremony with chanting, prayer and the calling in of the directions.

It was a mystical afternoon. Just as we were starting, whales began to breach against the light of the setting sun a few hundred yards offshore.

Our labyrinth had a one-way path. It was like a meandering spiral to the center. Once in the middle, we each paused to place our offering at the altar, and returned the same way.

While walking the labyrinth I heard:

> *Forgiveness is the empty space between judgment and innocence.*

Forgiveness is the return to innocence.

What we hide defines us. What we share frees us.

Go into the empty space.

The Vision Quest participants slowly walked in one by one. As they moved to the center, they were instructed to ask themselves to be shown whom to forgive.

Then, when the persons to forgive were revealed in their mind's eye, they would open their heart to connect with them with compassion, and recite a forgiveness prayer.

As they moved away from the center, they came face to face with everyone with whom they had journeyed for the past week.

It was amazing to watch the intimate encounters as they embraced and shared their hearts with one another.

Just before I got to the center, I looked into the eyes of and embraced a fellow participant who is every bit *The Man - Evolved*. In his embrace, I closed my eyes and let go.

I began to experience a tingling and opened my eyes. I felt Love, Joy.

As I did, I experienced everything melt into space. It was like everything was made of tiny grains of sand: the beach, the waves, the people, and the sky.

Now a great gust of slow wind was dissolving everything into a vortex of energy, like water flowing into an invisible drain in the space before me.

I soon found myself in a place of absolute nothingness.

There were no walls and nothing to see or feel. Everything was light and completely void of color. There was less than nothing present, and I had no awareness of any form of any kind, including me.

I was so far into nothingness, I heard myself say in an echo:

"I am so far away, I do not know where I came from."

   "Where did I come from," a distant part of me replied.

From the labyrinth

"What labyrinth?"

It was then that the labyrinth began to come back into form by way of tiny particles drawn together by the point of my awareness. It was happening meticulously from complete innocence.

I was observing external form being recreated from within, like sand falling backward from every direction onto the beach to perfectly form what already was, but reFraming my view of it.

In this moment, I knew everything we experience is a replication of our perspective. We can choose to reFrame our life simply by playing in the sandbox of forgiveness.

It became clear to me, when we are suffering, we are stuck in an old tale which is seems so believable we take it as truth – even though the story is nothing but tiny particles held together by thought and old emotion.

I saw how we could use forgiveness to shift the illusion of suffering into love, like pulling the foundation out from underneath a towering skyscraper. Everything collapses into the empty space below.

EVERYTHING.

And, when we are clear of the shame connected to our old story, suddenly **there is nothing to forgive**.

Incredibly, our memory also shifts to reflect our new truth, our new myth.

The old story is gone with the wind.

On the beach in the labyrinth, I experienced the nectar of *evolutionary forgiveness*.

Evolutionary Forgiveness

The Recognition that Memory is ReFramed Through Forgiveness.

The Ability of One Person to Shift All Their Relationship Dynamics Through Forgiveness.

The Creation of a New Myth for All.

What if
forgiveness was
easy and fun?

Would more
people practice
forgiveness?

All is Provided For Now

What if millions began clearing shame?

How quickly
could Earth
become Sarza?

ReFrame Nine

Bending Time & Space

How Powerful Are We Humans?

It's supposed to be the Fool's second-to-last day in Mexico. It has been an extraordinary trip.

The Vision Quest is over, and he can really let go and relax.

He is exhilarated and exhausted. He walks the beach. His awareness drifts back to the wedding in Hawaii just a few months prior - the Sacred Union ceremony.

Each person performed the union of their own Divine Feminine and Divine Masculine energies. Back then the Fool remembered he really hadn't known what the ceremony was all about – but it had felt right, and he had trusted his community. Going to Hawaii was something of a Choiceless Choice.

Now as he walks up the hill to the house to receive a deep tissue massage from a friend, he feels a completion of some sort and wonders what it's all about.

Lying on the table a few minutes later, he speaks to the masseuse about meeting Judith Ray. He relates his experiences of the six-week trip here in Mexico back to the ceremony in Hawaii and swimming with the dolphins. He also mentions he met someone here in Mexico, but she is returning to her home in Florida tomorrow. He felt something in her presence, but hadn't acted on it.

His friend works her elbow deep into his ribcage.

Something about the combination of the elbow and what he is feeling about the entire trip triggers deep, raw emotion. The Fool begins to cry. He cannot stop. He is convulsing.

The tears have arrived.

His friend keeps working on his body. She knows how to hold space for the transformation she senses.

For nearly half an hour, he sobs. It comes in waves, in between laughter and words. The mood is light, and yet he grieves.

I can see he is both connected to the Father, and grounded in the Mother. The cords of light from above and below are present. I watch as remnants of his maroon flame rise into his chest and merge with the brilliant white light of his expanding heart to form a tunnel of sorts, a passage.

There is a deep alchemy happening, as the suppressed fear and shame are being converted into love. He has felt it before, many times – but never like this. I observe his entire energetic body take on the shape of a morphogenetic field. He looks younger, vibrant and alive.

From a passage in his heart, a brilliant ray of light moves through time and space towards the beach, a 15-minute walk away over dirt roads and through the jungle. The ray of light arcs above the jungle like a rainbow and falls upon two women enjoying their last day together in the ocean.

Suddenly one says to the other: "I have to stay."

"Yes you do." replies her friend, while watching her run out of the breaking waves.

"I'll be back."

The woman grabs her clothes and begins to run toward the house where she had met a man a week before. She had felt something in his presence, but hadn't been ready to explore it yet.

Now she is.

She is barefoot on the trail, running through the jungle as fast as she can.

Meanwhile, the massage is over. The masseuse is leaving. Just before she walks out the door, the Fool says to her, "Maybe now since I let all that go, she will stay."

He lies back on the table to rest. He is alone.

A few minutes later, a knocking stirs him.

As the door opens slowly, his view is obscured by the expanding silhouette of a figure created by the bright afternoon light shining into the house.

The figure slowly emerges from the orange and yellow glow.

Suddenly she is standing there, sweating and breathing like she'd run all the way up the hill from the beach.

They look into each other's eyes. The afternoon light is cascading around her like angel's wings.

She is perfect.

I know what no one else knows; this man will need this woman for what lies ahead, and both will need one another later in ways they cannot imagine now.

Pushing himself off the table to his feet, the Fool asks: "What are you doing?"

"I have come to change my ticket. I want to stay with you. Would that be alright?"

Their smiles awaken together as the answer is already understood in the space between them. The woman jumps into the Fool's arms, her arms and legs embracing him.

For the next three days, the couple explores their hearts. It is like they have known each other forever.

He calls her, *Evermore*.

She calls him *Eternal*.

Their union seems to be oddly and magically self-organized without any effort, and they decide to spend more time together back in Colorado.

At the Sky Temple after returning from Mexico, Evermore and Eternal are playing a card game with his young daughter.

His daughter goes on a six-game losing streak. The frustration is obvious. She asks to play one more game to try and win. It's a game that is impossible to lose on purpose and Eternal watches helplessly as she loses once more.

The young girl is overtaken by emotion, and becomes unresponsive to her father's requests. She turns away from them, head down, and shoulders slouched.

Eternal closes his eyes and begins to practice deep listening in the space. He shifts his entire awareness to his heart, and goes deep inside to feel the emotion, both present in himself and his child.

There is nothing else he can do but love her, as she runs downstairs. He has witnessed this in her before, and is deeply curious about her process.

He tiptoes down the stairs and peers around the corner. Evermore is just behind, witnessing.

The girl is shaking and rocking back and forth with a far off look in her eyes, as though in a trance. He knows she is safe, as he feels the truth of the situation. Staying in his heart, he sends her love through intention.

I AM with them too. Our hearts are entrained.

We are One, together.

Moments later, I notice Eternal watching as the girl submits to her heart and sobs. I see a great release, although to a fool it would appear she is in trauma.

I AM Sarza.

I AM the Great Mother, and I AM Nature.

When Eternal feels she is ready, he goes to her slowly with open arms. She embraces her father deeply. The crying continues.

I AM Provider of All, and I AM always with you.

Play and be free in your heart.

After a while, Eternal offers to read his daughter a bedtime story. She accepts, running freely off to grab a favorite. There is lightness in her not seen before.

Before reading the story, while she is lying next to Evermore, Eternal asks her what happened after she left the game.

"I don't know what happened, or how I got there, Daddy. Suddenly I was just kind of stuck. But then, I had a breakthrough."

Satisfied with her answer for the moment, Eternal and Evermore read her a story about how a young girl gives everything away and then receives everything she needs. Everyone falls asleep together after reading.

The next afternoon in the car heading to town, Eternal asks his daughter, "How did you break through Sweetheart?"

"I opened the gate of my heart and went into a passage," she says. "It was really scary going in."

How did you open the gate?

"I stopped worrying."

"Do you worry about me?" he asks.

"I used to — until last night," she answers. "I used to try and help you in your problems. But now I know they are not real."

"What do you mean — they aren't real?" her father inquires with great curiosity.

"You always have what you need, Daddy. Everyone does. You just have to feel all the way inside your heart, so you can see what is real and what is not."

"You are amazing — my greatest teacher," I say.

"And you know what, Dad? It's just like that story we read last night. It's the greatest gift. You just have to let go of what's not real to get what you really need. I want to share this gift with everyone, because when one person has a breakthrough, so does everybody."

"Yes," says Eternal. "You have an extraordinary gift Sweetheart, don't forget it when get you older like your Dad did — no matter what anyone says."

"Okay." she replies.

Later, Evermore, Eternal and his three daughters are leaving a store downtown. It's a quiet Sunday. The kids were scheduled to be with their mother, but in a strange turn of events, we all find ourselves together.

We are all having a great time.

We are connected.

It's dark when we step into the night. A line of cars is passing us from the left. We pause on the sidewalk together in front of the three-lane street.

After the cars pass, the street appears deserted, except for one car coming from the right. It looks like a moving shadow.

Together, we step out into the empty lane waiting for the far lane to clear. Our car is parked directly opposite us on the other side of the street.

As the car gets closer, we take a few steps toward the center lane and all pause. A **maroon** automobile is approaching. We notice the driver.

"Really?" wonders the fool.

"How curious," muses the Fool.

Yes, it is so.

Suddenly, there is a blur to our left. Instinctively, we know, it's Eternal's seven year-old daughter. She is running unseen toward our parked car - directly into the path of the car driven by the Shadow.

There is no time to intervene. Impact is imminent.

The reality of the accident instantly becomes clear to the fool. It's the end. The car is moving swiftly and is almost against her small body.

> I remain completely neutral and totally present to our responsibility. The Shadow is here because I left the door to our relationship slightly ajar without clear resolution.

> *I AM Sarza, the self-organizing field.*

> *I keep everything in perfect order… the forests, the stars, the planets, and the galaxies.*

> *When you connect to Me, your life easefully falls into natural order because I AM Divine perfection.*

> *Go now and carve new pathways.*

In this moment of expanded awareness, we decide to stake our intent powerfully. We choose Grace, and a larger perspective.

Our energy expands together: Eternal, Evermore and daughters. Our hearts link up, and everything slows down around us. Time is nearly standing still.

We have become one morphogenetic field. Lights are descending from Father Sky above and ascending from Mother Earth below.

With a force of tremendous clarity, I focus our collective intent on the few inches of emptiness between the bumper and the small girl.

Everything we have goes dynamically and powerfully toward maintaining this tiny gap.

We see a bit of safe space beyond the moving vehicle, and we energetically push her there with all our intent.

Suddenly time speeds back up. Tires screech.

Eternal's daughter's hand touches the parked car. Her body follows and flattens against the door.

The car stops in the space where she was.

She is safe.

We gather the family and move everyone away from the incident. Before leaving, Eternal pauses to turn towards the Shadow. He bows with hands in prayer position and a nod of thanks.

Internally, he says powerfully: "Thank you for the lessons and gifts. You are no longer in my now - be dismissed."

I AM clear, resolute.

I have nothing, but gratitude.

The entire experience seemed to be oddly and magically self-organized without any effort on my part.

Later the girl would say,

> *"Dad, I never saw it coming."*

All is Provided For Now.

Evermore Eternal AM I.

After reframing, what happens to suffering?

Do reFramed problems still exist?

If suffering is optional, do we need a savior?

Perhaps Christ has already returned to Earth a Fool?

Thank you for reading **ReFrame.**

Please visit **www.lifeisheart.org** to learn more about reFraming 'success' and contributing to the evolution of a heart-centered human consciousness.

All is Provided for Now

Sarza

Appendix

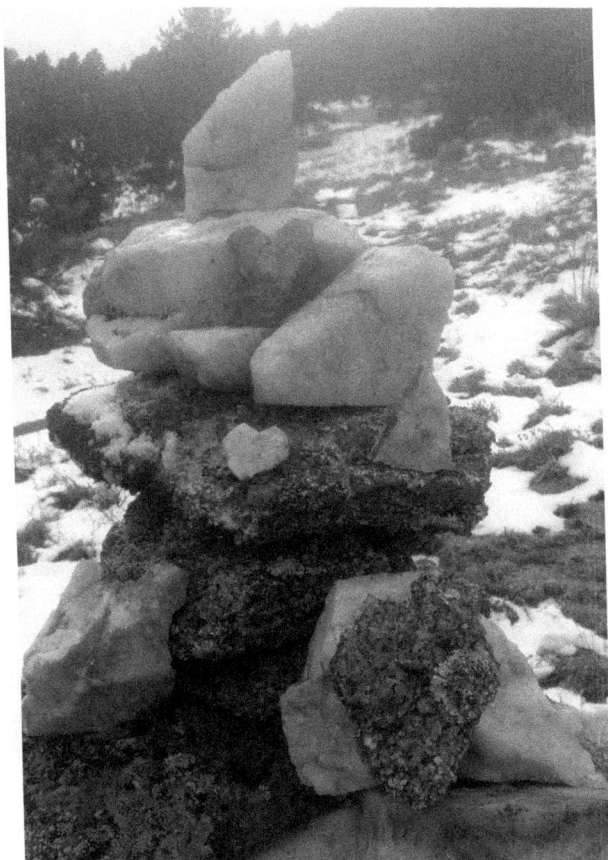

Sky Temple Forgiveness Alter

How to Lower SPAM

Punish children.

Dislike your parents, or anyone.

Bicker, blame, brag, confront or gossip.

Make people wrong or manipulate outcomes.

Begin with, "You, I should, or I am supposed to."

Have concern about the news, politics, or fairness.

Ask why, whine, complain, criticize, or keep secrets.

Keep score, stockpile, judge anyone, or complain.

Give advice without listening, or be a victim.

Lie, take it personally, or talk over people.

Apply moral standards, or justify anger.

Dislike your parents, or anyone.

Punish children.

A Simple Shame Clearing Exercise:

Walk into a wooded area until you find a tree that you love. Embrace the tree, pressing your stomach to the bark and feeling the vertical energy present. Imagine the crown of your head, your belly and the soles of your feet are open to energy flowing through them. Ask Father Sky to rain love upon you, and Mother Earth and the tree to extract your shame. Allow the energy from above to filter down through your body pressing out the shame through your abdomen and the soles of your feet. Let go & open the heart to magic.

Deep Listening Group Questions

<u>FN</u>: What is meaning of: "It's not personal, never was & never will be"?

<u>Zero</u>: Which global paradigms do the Fool & his Father represent? Is it possible to shift reality with love?

<u>One</u>: Feel and describe your greatest wish coming true. What happens to your SPAM when you do?

<u>Two</u>: What is Sarza? Explore a mystical experience you've had.

<u>Three</u>: Describe being punished from a child's perspective. Explore the Power Paradox; how can we live the truth of it?

<u>Four</u>: Can you feel your Shame Basket? Do you have secrets you're ready to reveal? What does the Christian Camp signify?

<u>Five</u>: Have you experienced Choiceless Choice? What true feelings have you held back in fear of hurting someone else?

<u>Sarza</u>: Who are Medicine Children? And why do we medicate them?

<u>Six</u>: Describe your frustrations with money, acceptance and/or love. What is the meaning of 'All is Provided For Now'?

<u>Seven</u>: When do you give up? How has nature blessed you? Be honest describing your relationships that are incomplete.

<u>Eight</u>: Are you waiting for forgiveness? Whose responsibility is it to forgive? Describe the space between judgment and innocence?

<u>Nine</u>: What is possible when many join hearts with mutual intent? What is the role of Christ / Christianity in the book?

ReFrame Affirmations

When Life Gets Hard, I Open My Heart - <u>*Zero*</u>

I Invite All Aspects Of My Soul To Return - <u>*One*</u>

When My SPAM Is Up, All Is Provided For - <u>*Two*</u>

I Create True Affluence By Feeling Good Now - <u>*Three*</u>

I AM In Charge Of My Perspective - <u>*Four*</u>

Sharing Authentic Feelings Creates Serendipity - <u>*Five*</u>

I AM Powerful When I Allow Myself to Feel - <u>*Six*</u>

When Life Gets Wonky, Nature Is My Guide - <u>*Seven*</u>

Forgiveness Is Recognition Of My Soul's Power - <u>*Eight*</u>

I AM Far More Powerful Than I Was Told - <u>*Nine*</u>

SPAM Boosters

<u>*Zero*</u> - *Artistically Garden, Indoors and Out*

<u>*One*</u> — *Get Rid of Everything You Don't Love — Truly*

<u>*Two*</u> - *Handwrite Thank You Notes to Your Minnie's*

<u>*Three*</u> - *Play Before Work, at Work, and After Work*

<u>*Four*</u> — *Tell the Absolute Truth & Build Incredible Altars*

<u>*Five*</u> - *Learn the Heart Language and Speak it Daily*

<u>*Six*</u> - *Take 100% Responsibility, 100% of the Time*

<u>*Seven*</u> - *Start a ReFrame Circle with People You Trust*

<u>*Eight*</u> — *Create Your Character & Sing Forgiveness Music*

<u>*Nine*</u> — *Visit Magical Places & Swim with Dolphins*

Colonial Hall

Sky Temple

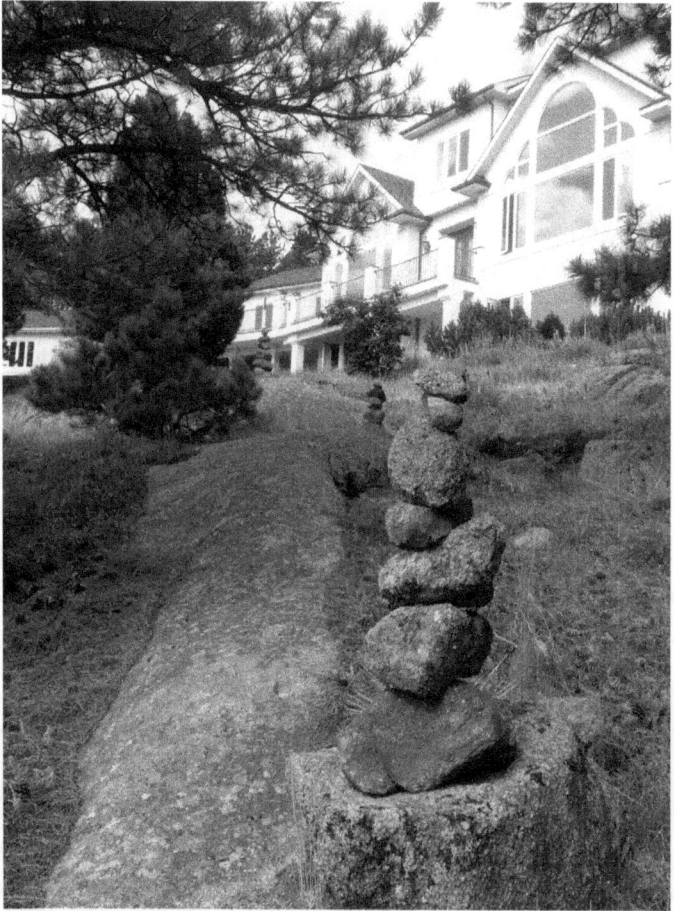

Special Thanks

To my White Birth Momma: Judith Gray Walton Smith, and to my daughters Eliza, Ava and Anya, what an honor.

To Heather L. Porter, for the courageous journey we shared, and for simply being the gift of Evermore.

To Denali Taos for revealing impeccable wisdom and standing with me all the way through.

To Parker, Steve and Travis— what a journey it was my brothers.

To the Sky Temple and my fabulous community of Paul, Reese, Stephen, and Lauren, plus Sharkey, Cydney, Gayatri, Matthew, Andy, Michelle – plus our guests. What blessings we share.

To Armand, Kate, Bettsee, Brittany, Chelli, Sina, Amanda, Nina, Katy, Brooks, Andrew, Tom, Joyous, Kasey, Bill, Heidi, Ashley, Alicia, David, Stacee, Tony, Dr. G, Becky, Dan, Jim, Barbara, Jeremy, Beth, George, Kait, Maribeth, Alaya, Brooke, LoveJoy, Calla, Dusty, Corwin, Gretchen, Kendra, Birgit, Cary, Zeona, Walter & all for showing up as a perfect cast of characters.

To the Good People of Nashville, TN – including Massood, Dina, Jamie, Anthoniji, Atul, Ed, Andrew, Robyn, Michael, Deborah, Ngawang, Jonathon, Jay, Elizabeth, Brandi, Tobi, Billy, Paul, Bill, Mac... and all for embracing my Foolish return.

To the Good People of Sayulita, Mexico – including Sipa, Organy, Diego, Danny, Paul, Val, Ed, Lesa, Rosaleo, Tomas, Linda, TR, Coral, John, Moises, Monica, and all for living in Joy.

To Mr. & Mrs. E. Dan Smith II, Alden, Elizabeth and all Walton's and Smith's for being an extraordinary support system.

www.ingramcontent.com/pod-product-compliance
Lightning Source LLC
LaVergne TN
LVHW051520080426
835509LV00017B/2131